IS A FOUR-
LETTER WORD

*A Mental Health Survival Guide
for Professionals*

by Andy Salkeld

First published in Great Britain by Practical Inspiration Publishing, 2020

ISBN   978-1-78860-155-9 (print)
        978-1-78860-157-3 (epub)
        978-1-78860-156-6 (mobi)

Practical Inspiration
PUBLISHING

CONTENTS

FOREWORD

David Chan, Inclusion and Diversity Partner at Squire Patton Boggs

Is life a four-letter word? This is perhaps debatable (an inevitable question coming from a pedantic lawyer).

It is definitely a six-letter word – finite. This is obvious to a lawyer working to six minute chargeable chunks of life… there is only so much time in a day.

Lawyers live increasingly busy lives in uncertain and challenging times. There is a constant and inexorable demand for us to be more knowledgeable, more speedy, more efficient and much more. We are also often portrayed as exhibiting unparalleled attention to detail, having expansive knowledge of every law in the country and in possession of Vulcan-like emotional armour.

Over recent years, there has been a growing concern across the legal industry about lawyer wellbeing and mental health. The issue is complex and is shaped by the individuality of each of our lives and other factors, such as disability, age, class, race, gender and sexuality.

A common thread, however, is a perceived stigma associated with admitting that one is suffering from mental health challenges. This book serves as an open and incisive view into the mind of a young professional, how life can unravel and how it can be turned round.

Each person's life is what they make of it. Life is not always easy, but it is easy in the pursuit of 'more' to be deflected from life itself. We sometimes forget about the real reasons for our existence until a significant jolt, which is often a four-letter word, forces us to reassess life.

I do hope that this book will empower its reader to reflect and refocus on the important things in life (and decide how many letters it comprises)…

A NOTE FROM CHRIS ETHERINGTON

Partner at RSM

When you are next sat at your desk at work, take a moment.

Look around.

If you work in an office environment, it's easy to think you know the people you work with. You probably spend most of your waking hours with your colleagues.

For some, you'll be spending more time with your teammates this week than with your family.

Do you truly know them?

Sure, you talk to each other all day. You may enjoy working with them and have a pretty good flavour of their personalities. There might even be a few you count as true friends.

I thought I knew Andy. The reality is I barely knew him at all.

We were in different departments at work and on different floors but every so often, the pair of us were thrown into the maelstrom of stress that is getting a transaction completed for a client.

Did I have a clue that Andy was struggling? Not a scooby.

I knew a version of him: Andy with the acceptable mask that he put on for work. I was wearing one too.

This book tears that mask away. It is a brutally honest account of what a career in a large accountancy firm can be like and the potential toll it can take on your mental health. A mental health survival guide for anyone starting out their careers in an accountancy firm.

As someone who has been through the ranks and has been fortunate enough to make it through to Partner, there is a lot in this book that rings true to me. The imposter syndrome is definitely still going strong (I'll get found out one day).

Thankfully, things are starting to change and there is a lot of good work being done by firms to promote mental health awareness now.

There's a long way to go but stories like this one help to break down the stigma associated with mental health that prevents us from being open and honest about our struggles in the workplace.

Not everyone's experience will be the same but I'm grateful that Andy's shared his. Hopefully one day we can all take off our masks.

A NOTE FROM JONATHAN EDGELEY

Corporate Partnership Director at MYNDS

During January 2007, my father led an intervention into my life.

I wasn't aware of anything that was going on around me. All I know is that I woke up in a rehabilitation centre in South Africa.

I didn't realise it at the time but this was to be the start of a new dawn.

Today, over a decade later, I am in recovery from alcohol and substance addiction.

I have a wonderful wife and four amazing children. My purpose in life has changed from seeking highs and feeding an addiction that was controlling me, to helping others who suffer with adverse mental health and addiction to access the appropriate help and support.

There are many phenomenal campaigns aimed at reducing the stigma of mental health and getting people to talk. The reality of it all is that the people openly talking about their mental health are not the ones who are struggling with it daily. Those talking have already found acceptance in themselves.

There is still a lot of work to be done to help others to accept themselves.

People are still dying from overdoses. Pain-killer addiction is increasing significantly. Suicide rates are at a sixteen-year high.

Mental health needs to be viewed in the same way as physical health.

We need more people talking about their own experiences of mental health illness, sharing them without concern of judgement, ridicule or fear for their career.

I have heard Andy speak of his story and the work he is doing first-hand. He speaks with absolute authenticity in a highly thought provoking and poignant way. His only agenda in any of his work – whether this book, his talks or anything else he does in life – is to carry the simple message of hope to those who are still suffering in silence.

It is a pleasure to be a part of Andy's journey and to help break the stigma around adverse mental health.

May these words and this book help encourage more people to talk openly.

PREFACE

I never thought I'd write a book.

If I'm honest, I never thought that I'd be alive and here today.

I always believed I would end my life at one point or another. It was always going to be: achieve something; feel the accomplishment that goes with it; then end things.

Every time I reached the place where I would write that full stop in my life, a wild semicolon appeared, and I just kept on going.

For many that semicolon doesn't appear to save them.

What gets left behind after a suicide is unimaginable. There are constant questions that can never be answered and an event that can never truly be understood. An unexplained hole is left in the heart of those around; one that can never heal.

There is no closure.

I don't want to end my life and leave anyone with that hole in theirs. I am going to keep fighting and keep doing what I can to show that living with depression is not only possible, but also worthwhile. People can overcome all forms of adversity, and suffering adverse mental health is no different.

This book will cover a lot of personal experiences that some may find hard to read or understand. I know that even mentioning some of these experiences to my family and friends is painful for them, so do not be scared if you feel uncomfortable or get upset.

I say what I do to be honest; to show what it's really like.

I don't want to be a hero.

I certainly don't want to be a martyr.

All I want is for those out there struggling to know that there is hope. There are ways through the darkest of times. There are ways you can recover and move beyond them.

Most importantly though, for anyone out there struggling, know that you are not alone.

The world can be overwhelming, but you don't have to face it by yourself.

No one does.

Andy Salkeld

just another guy

ACKNOWLEDGEMENT

There were many people who were there for me when I was in my darkest place. There are far too many to name and I wouldn't be able to do any of them the justice they truly deserve.

This acknowledgement isn't for them.

This book is for my absolute best friend ever, whom I love to bits and who means the complete fucking world to me. Like everyone, we've had our ups and downs, been closer and further apart; but we've stuck by one another through all the shit life has thrown at us over the years and whenever we are together it is like no time has passed and nothing has changed.

She inspires me daily to keep writing and telling my story; helping others in a way I never thought would be possible for me. She shows me that no matter how shit the world might be and no matter how shit either of us might feel, there are no problems in this world that can't be solved by two people sharing a pint in a pub.

She won't believe a word of this, but it's true.

Here's to you.

X

So, what did you make of LIFE on the front cover?

Was it 'SHIT'? Were you thinking 'FUCK'?

Or did you happen to see 'THIS' and 'LUCK' after a while?

Funny how we tend to see the negatives rather than searching for the positives.

Some will argue that the tiles are laid out in such a way to make you only see 'SHIT' and 'FUCK' and that this is unfair. I'm sorry to tell you this, but life is unfair. No one is going to tell you what the right answer is. No one is going to make life easy for you. It's entirely up to you to make what you want of your life and to fight for what you believe in.

You can choose to live with 'SHIT' and keep thinking 'FUCK', or you can stand up for yourself and believe there is a way through it all to find something slightly more positive. Sure, it's not an easy journey and life will probably try to block you along the way. But you can do it.

It just takes time.

Those who like a good puzzle: take another look at the front cover. Your opponent has played LIFE as the first word on the Scrabble board. Your seven tiles are scattered in front of you: S H T _ U C K. Can you score a bonus fifty points by using all seven tiles in a single turn, adding them to the letters already played to form a new word?

You can.

A couple of ways in fact.

The answers are hidden in the book somewhere.

Happy hunting.

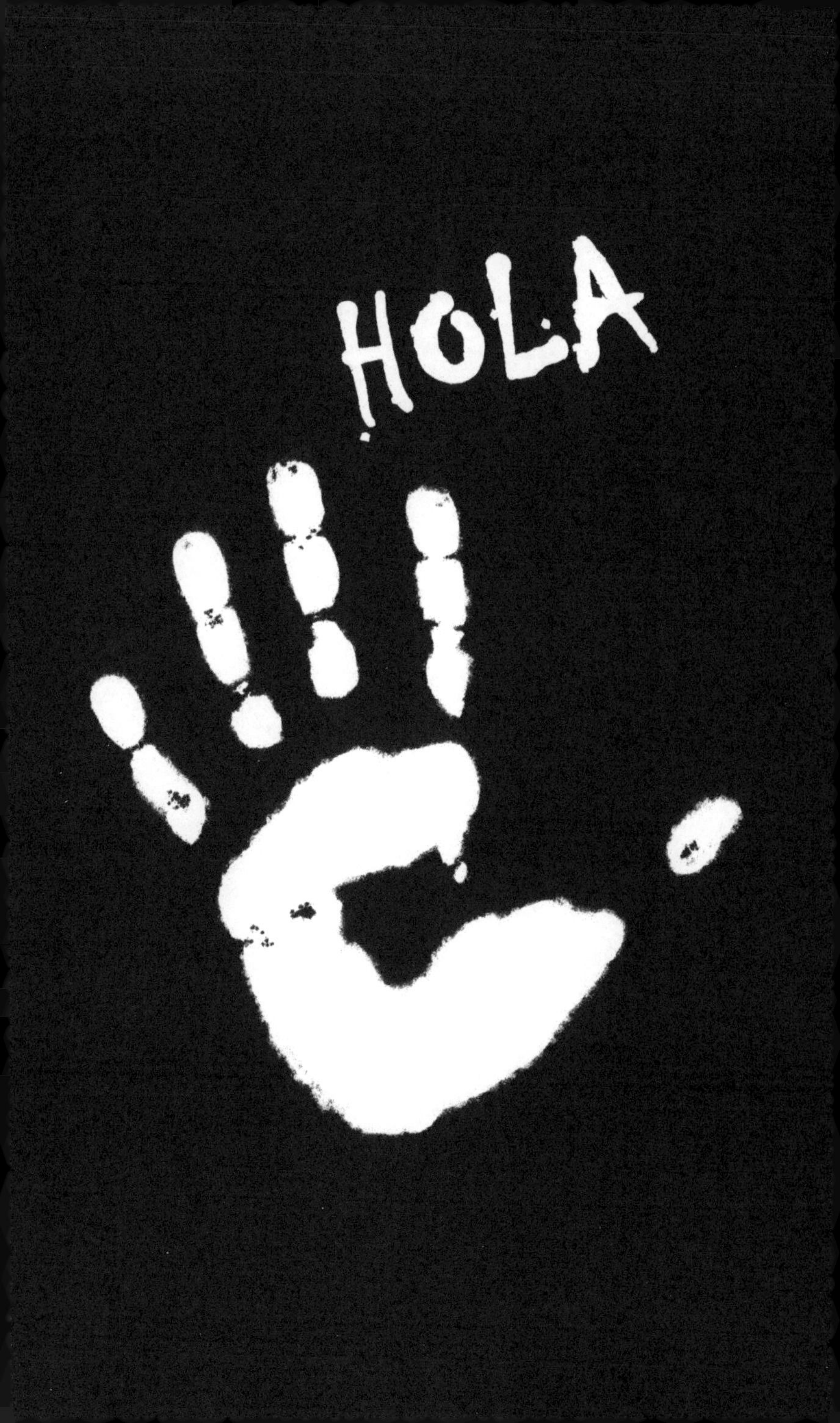
HOLA

ONE

MY OWN WORST ENEMY

Understanding Mental Health

HARD

What do you do when one of your colleagues calls in sick?

'Hey. I can't come into work today. I've got one hell of a cold and just need to rest,' they say in a snotty voice with a weak cough in between the words!

No worries. We'll be okay. You focus on getting better. Don't want anyone else catching it anyway. Insert generic 'feel better' comment. Hang up the phone and then be done with it.

Whatever.

But what if it carries on?

It turns out it isn't just a cold. It is something far more serious. Maybe bacterial meningitis; from malnourishment and poor living conditions.

You get a message through saying that they've been taken to the hospital; a big building with patients, but that's not important right now. They'll likely be there for a few weeks as they are treated, cared for and monitored.

You organise a sympathy card, maybe even some flowers, once again reiterating the platitudes of 'get well soon'. You then go about organising other people in the team to cover their work whilst they recover.

It's a pain, but you'd want to be treated the same way if you were in hospital.

When they finally make it back into the office, they're likely greeted with a 'welcome back' card or maybe an embarrassing 'we missed you' banner hung over their desk. They are told to take it easy and ease back into things slowly. The first few days in the office are probably mostly them just retelling the story of how sick they were, what it was like in hospital and how they have recovered since.

Eventually everything returns to normal. Maybe with you all learning some life lessons about how to better care for yourselves.

But what if you received a different phone call?

'Hey. I can't come into work today. I'm feeling really anxious and self-conscious and am finding it hard to concentrate.' There is a whimper in their voice, sounding uncertain as to whether you'll even understand what they're saying.

Or how about?

'Hey. I can't come into work today. I'm really stressed with the workload and I'm just struggling with everything.'

What about?

'Hey. I don't think I should come to work today. I'm feeling suicidal right now and the thought of seeing people is too much. It took all my strength just to make this phone call.' Then the phone line simply goes dead without anything else being said.

Have you ever had one of these phone calls?

How would you respond to it?

Now imagine if you never received a phone call. No communication at all. What would be your first thought?

What would you feel if you found out days, weeks, maybe months later that your colleague had committed suicide? They didn't feel confident enough to call you that morning when things were bad. Their spiral of depression was in overdrive. They felt they would be judged.

Why do we treat these things any differently at all?

Mental health is just as important as physical health.

The reason is one of stigma.

What do you think would happen if you told your manager or leadership team at work that you lived with depression?

Do you think it would be the death knell for your career? I did. Do you think you'd be looked down upon? I did. Do you think about whether you'd be given the same opportunities as others? I did.

I was terrified of all the above. It made my depression and anxiety worse!

This stigma attached to mental health is pervasive throughout our culture. It is present in our businesses. It is present in our politics. It is ever present and only now are we starting to make small steps to break it down.

I'm not here to change the world.

I can't do that alone.

I'm too lazy.

I'm here to tell a story.

I'm not going to impart any ancient wisdom to you. I'm not going to tell you any secrets. This isn't a 'get rich quick' script for the soul.

Everything I talk about you'll probably already know.

I'm just willing to say it.

SAME

No two people are alike.

Everyone is an individual.

Here's the first of probably many forays into my love of science and maths. I'm not going to shy away from it! We're starting with a good one though. This is about special relativity! Thank you, Albert Einstein!

Ever heard of the twins paradox?[1] Probably not. It's a thought experiment about special relativity. One twin remains on earth whilst the other identical twin is accelerated into space incredibly fast only to return to the planet sometime later. Under the principles of relativity and time dilation, each twin should find the other to have aged less; however, contrary to this, only the twin who travelled into space aged less.

I won't go into the details of why. That'd probably take a few books just to scratch the surface!

The answer is simply, physics!

---

[1] www.einstein-online.info/spotlights/Twins.1.html Accessed on 30/08/19

What's interesting though is that NASA recently conducted a similar experiment[2] to investigate the impact of living in space for a prolonged period. A pair of twins were studied over the course of a year, where one lived in space orbiting our little blue planet, whilst the other stayed at home on the ground. At the end of the year it was observed that there was a seven percent difference in gene expression.

That seven percent difference is just from living under different conditions.

Nature and nurture make each of us unique.

Just as we're all unique, so are our minds. Each of us has our own unique brain chemistry.

Notice how even here I refer to it as a chemistry; the science of the physical.

Our brains may be physical constructs of water, neurons, synapses and all that grey stuff that I don't really like thinking about, but our minds are certainly more than that. We still don't fully understand where our thoughts and emotions come from, or where our memories are stored. When we can't even understand the simpler side of the mind then it's no wonder that we are so far away from making the same strides within the arena of mental health as we have made within physical health over the previous decades.

You can talk about it, listen to stories, attend seminars and even read shitty little books like this one; but without experience it is so hard to make sense of it all.

---

[2] www.nasa.gov/twins-study Accessed on 30/08/19

I certainly didn't understand it until I lived it!

SHOW

I'm going to tell you my story.

There are people out there who tell their heroic journeys of overcoming physical disabilities, undergoing tremendous hardships and surviving experiences that pushed their bodies to the very limits of humanity.

I'm going to do the same! I'm going to tell you my story!

It's a bit shit though.

It's far from heroic. I'm an accountant!

The only hardships I really faced are those I put on myself.

The only limits I broke were for speeding to make sure I made it to meetings on time.

It's really fucking boring.

So why am I even bothering to tell it then?

Well, I almost killed myself.

Yep.

Starting at the almost end.

I almost killed myself. I almost couldn't tell my story. I don't think I'd trust anyone else to tell my story the way I would want it told; not that anyone would really want to tell my story anyway. They certainly wouldn't think of casting Nathan Fillion as the real me and Ryan Reynolds as my twisted alter ego inner voice, in some poor rehashing of *Fight Club*.

The first rule of being an accountant is to never admit you're an accountant.

More importantly, when I finally told the world that I had almost ended my life, so many people said that they had no idea. They didn't know that I was struggling. They didn't know the pain I was in. They couldn't tell what was going on in my head. Not for not wanting to care for me, but because I hid it all away.

I wore my mask every day.

I hid the truth behind fake smiles, fake fashion, fake laughter, fake confidence, fake chauvinism and fake stories of success. I was a fake and no one knew.

I tell my story to show others what can be happening underneath the surface. I tell my story for all those out there feeling the way I did at various points of my life and career, so that they can know they are not alone. I tell it so that people around those who may be struggling, pause occasionally simply to just check in with them.

And finally, last but by no means least, I tell my story because I really fucking love the sound of my own voice!

Our Inner Voices, Critics and Conversations

TALK

We all talk to ourselves.

Right now, as you read this sentence, you are talking to yourself. If you've met me, or heard one of my talks, you're probably hearing this in my dulcet tones; along with the stupid intonation and emphasis I put on different words. If you haven't and know who Nathan Fillion is, then you are hopefully hearing it in his luxurious and eloquent voice as that's who I said would be cast as me in the movie of my miserable life. If neither of these is the case, you are probably just hearing your voice.

Talking to ourselves is how we think.

It's not bad!

It's not wrong!

It's just us saying to ourselves things like 'I fancy a cup of tea', encouraging us to go make one, or maybe 'I can smell cat litter', encouraging us to clean it. We have evolved beyond just basic instincts and this thought and communication with ourselves internally is a natural part of our lives now.

My hope for our journey together through this book is to demonstrate that those who struggle with adverse mental health, like I do with depression and occasionally anxiety, are no different from anyone else.

The difference is one of subtlety.

The inner monologues for those with adverse mental health may be a little louder, perhaps a little more frequent or maybe even pre-disposed to certain emotions such as fear in the case of anxiety or sadness in the case of depression.

Once you get to know your inner monologue and how they respond and react to things, it becomes a lot easier to control them, or at least manage them.

LOUD

We aren't a happy species.

We aren't happy people.

We are never content and always want more.

Whenever we say something is impossible, we make it possible. Whenever we say something cannot be done, we somehow find a way. We believe in pushing our boundaries. It's an inspiration to see the growth and success humanity has had over the years I've been alive. Sure, we've messed things up pretty catastrophically as a species as well, but we've exceeded every limit we've ever placed on ourselves.

It's impressive!

Feel good about yourself and pat yourself on the back for being human.

Now feel bad about it because we're the reason the planet is dying.

Swings and roundabouts.

Stepping back from humanity, we also like to push our own boundaries as individuals. It may not be as continuous or as often, but we always like to believe that we can do just that little better. We strive for greatness.

When was the last time you sat down and said to yourself that you were happy with what you achieved? Or where you are in life?

We rarely congratulate ourselves.

Take a moment to just feel what you have accomplished today, this week, this month or even this year!

You've made it here, so be proud of it.

Shout about it.

Celebrate it.

Or maybe just keep quiet about it and hope someone else recognises it and says something nice, then when they don't slowly slide into bitter resentment and passive aggression.

Your choice.

Sadly though, regardless of our successes, that drive within us to do better and achieve more manifests by telling us what we could have done better. Sometimes our thoughts on this are quiet. Sometimes they are loud. Sometimes they can be overwhelming. Regardless, that human drive for success and overcoming the impossible is there.

My inner monologue is always telling me I could do better and is always making me feel like I could do more!

You'll get to meet him soon enough.

CARE

The thing is though, even though we are our own loudest critic and do put a hell of a lot of undue pressure on ourselves, we do this for our own benefit and because we are looking out for ourselves.

The reason we internally debate so much of what we want to do, or what we could have done, is because we care for ourselves and care for our wellbeing. We know that the decisions we make can have consequences and therefore try to understand what will happen before it does. We try to protect ourselves from harm rather than experiencing it first-hand.

Consider this: you have worked late every night for a week and then finally make it to the weekend; your precious weekend! You just want to collapse in exhaustion. Your friends insist you go out, but your body is telling you to stay in. You want to see your friends, but your body is saying no and that you should rest.

More than likely you will end up seeing your friends and not giving your body and mind the time they need to recuperate. The fear of missing out is real!

Most of the internal conversations we have with ourselves revolve around whether we're making the right decision or not.

Spoiler alert: there is no right decision.

There is only a decision.

Whether it is right or not is entirely subjective and what you perceive as right won't necessarily be seen the same way by others. Focus less on whether it is the objective 'right decision' and more on whether it is a decision you are happy and comfortable about making.

It doesn't matter what other people think.

It only matters what you think.

And what you feel.

LONG

Our inner monologue is with us from when we begin to understand language up until the day we die. The volume, pitch and tone might change over time but that inner monologue is always there with us.

When I started going through my divorce, I found it incredibly difficult to separate the 'I' from the 'We'. I hadn't defined myself as an individual for over a decade and didn't know or understand what being an individual meant anymore. I had to teach myself that it was no longer 'our house' by default and it was 'my house'.

That's when I started speaking to my inner monologue again.

That's when I began to realise that 'I' was still a 'We', it was just with someone else.

One of my closest friends – honestly, the most beautiful and kindest person I have ever met – told me that I needed to rebuild the relationship I had with myself. That the relationship we have with ourselves is the longest relationship we'll ever have.

So, I started spending time alone.

Or not really alone.

I don't know.

I struggle a lot with loneliness, as I believe many of us do. When I heard this, it took a little while for it to sink in and for me to realise how true it is. I am in a relationship with myself. Sometimes it's a theoretical-threesome and there's another person involved, but when there's no other person, I am still able to keep myself company.

My company might not be great, but it's still company!

Spending time on the relationship you have with yourself is incredibly important.

I'm not talking about any kinky autoerotic asphyxiation fantasies, but there's certainly nothing wrong with them. You do you after all.

I'm talking about the emotional and mental sides of your relationship with yourself. Only through knowing yourself will you be able to connect with others in an honest and meaningful way.

BEST

Many of us have best friends.

That one person you can always count on.

Our best friends can change through time though.

Often when in a romantic relationship, your romantic partner will become your best friend. It's why breakups hurt a lot; you lose two people in one. You lose your romantic partner and your best friend. Recovering from this can take a long time as you no longer have the person you once relied upon for support during times like these.

Sometimes romantic relationships can blossom from best friendships. It can be complex to rewind and find the lust and passion that comes with new romance, but the rewards are without limits. This is what I felt I had found with my ex-wife. These relationships should last a lifetime as you already know that they're there for you no matter what and will be with you till the bitter end. Sadly, it didn't work out for us, but the circumstances were out of our control.

You have another best friend in your inner monologue.

Your inner monologue will never leave your side. They'll fight every fight with you. They'll look out for you during the best of times and worst of times. They truly are a best friend.

However, we must treat our inner monologue with respect, just as we would a best friend. They will treat us with the same respect in kind.

Would you really let your best friend wallow in self-pity for weeks?

Would you let your best friend beat themselves up over a poor grade?

Would you let anyone treat your best friend like shit?

I really hope you're answering no to all these questions, otherwise you probably need to re-evaluate your status as a best friend!

I get told that I need to be kinder to myself. I get told that I need to be less bothered about what other people think about me and focus more on what I think and believe about myself.

I get told that I need to love myself.

It's hard.

I'm still no good at it. I won't lie. I still consider myself a failure. I still believe I haven't achieved anything in my life.

I still don't treat myself or my inner monologue with the respect of a best friend. But I am trying to get better at it.

And that is all I can ask from you.

Start getting to know yourself some more. Start listening to yourself some more. Start caring about yourself some more. Becoming best friends with someone takes time and effort.

However, the sooner you start, the sooner it'll happen and that's when you can start beginning to find real acceptance in yourself.

Introductions

BOOK

This book is a strange one.

It's about my life and my experiences, but it's also so much more. There's no easy way to describe it or categorise it. Like all of us, it is beautifully unique.

If you've reached this far, that's great! It's certainly better than I do when reading books without lots of pictures. Throughout the remaining chapters of this book, we're going to follow the narrative of my life as a working adult in the professional service industry.

It is as boring as it sounds!

Luckily, I'm less boring than your average professional service industry worker!

Or so I tell myself at least.

Whilst I will often refer to my life as an accountant and working in professional practice, please don't feel that this book isn't for you if you don't. This book is relevant to all working adults. Life is busy. We could all use a bit of perspective at times. Use this book as a tool to help you find your perspective when you need it!

Assuming you still want to keep reading, here's what to expect as you head into each chapter.

Chapter Two covers a lot of background and theory that I reluctantly learned when I was a younger and more naive individual. It is now the cornerstone for a lot of how I live my life and how I interact with others daily.

Chapters Three through Six cover the early stages of my career. These are chapters of raw experience where I discovered that life wasn't all that I thought it was going to be. This is where this 'guy with spikes' ended up with some smoother edges and definitely some unneeded curves as middle-aged spread kicked in!

Chapter Seven is the big one. This is where I cover the depth of my depression and my suicidal thoughts. It is a searingly honest account of what depression can do to a person and what the edge of your world can look like. It's bleak. It's dark. It's miserable. But at least there's beer!

Chapters Eight and Nine are the beginnings of 'a life after almost ending'. They cover some key concepts that I now hold dear to me. This is where I discovered my purpose and it certainly wasn't what I thought it was. I learned that I want to help people grow through sharing my experiences and failures. I want to guide people through the storm that is life and help them become the heroes of their own story.

Kind of poetic.

Kind of sappy.

Kind of makes me a little sick in my mouth re-reading it.

It's all true.

Hopefully this gives you just enough to tempt you into reading further, without spoiling too much of the rollercoaster along the way.

ANDY

This is me.

This is my voice.

Or Nathan Fillion's. That's your choice.

You already know a lot about me and what my story will entail from reading the blurb, the Preface, the Foreword, the Notes From and even bits of this chapter. I don't want to reiterate those parts now as they'll be told in a lot more detail throughout the remainder of the book.

Plus, they're really boring. Who wants to hear about the life of an accountant?

I say accountant.

I'm not 'just' an accountant anymore.

I am an accountant, investor and director at a technology company based in Leeds. That bit is true. I also do a lot more work outside of that with helping corporate organisations, professional practices and individuals build mentally healthy cultures. I regularly tour, giving my keynote speech titled 'Breaking the Stigma'. I get involved in seminars, panels and more, trying to show that you can be more than your illness. I also seem to have written a book on it all. Have I told you about that? Have you read it? I do all of this and more for no other reason than to help people.

I will not shy away from being myself in this writing. I will write as myself, using the language I use every day. I won't try to put on a different style. I won't try to use a different tone of voice. This is me as if I was talking to you face-to-face over a coffee. It's me as if I was standing in front of an audience giving a talk. There's a modicum of thought that goes into what I write to not land me in legal trouble, but not much.

I also want to make it clear that whilst I will be challenging the decisions I made throughout my career and challenging the organisations and the fundamental ethos behind their practices, I do not hold any ill will at all. Regardless of how the decisions I made turned out for me, I would not make any different decisions. I have the utmost respect for the places I worked and the people I have worked with over the years. Just because it wasn't right for me doesn't mean it isn't right for you or for anyone else.

I am going to refrain from using names of any individuals and organisations throughout this book. I am going to talk about bullying, poor leadership and inappropriate work behaviour. This is not a witch hunt, so telling you their names isn't important.

Finally, I am not going to shy away from any sides of my personality. In breaking the stigma of mental health and what it means, you need to be willing to show all of yourself. I will make incredibly niche references to things I like. You may have noticed already that some of the chapter titles and subchapter titles refer to pop punk and ska music. There will be references to video games, cartoons and movies, some of which I might not even know I'm making. What is important though is that this is the truest representation of me.

After finishing this book, I would hope that you know me. I would hope you feel you know the real me as an individual and could probably even recall some of the ridiculous stories I'll share.

I believe that for us all to create mentally healthy cultures in our businesses and practices we need to be able to be true and honest to ourselves and each other. We need to stop wearing our masks and just be ourselves and accept who we are.

This is my attempt to show you that some chartered accountant, corporate financier, business intelligence specialist, finance director, investor and co-owner of multiple companies – who on paper looks incredibly successful – is actually just another geeky mathematician without any confidence who has an eclectic taste in music, loves playing video games, quotes way too much *Star Wars*, remembers way too much about Pokémon and has numerous tattoos he designed himself referring to all the above!

SELF

Don't waste your time listening to me when I'm going to introduce you to the voice inside my head.

> *"Are you making a Blink-182 reference here? Wait, people can see this? Are you sure you want people to see me? It's on you if this goes wrong! You know what I'm like."*

I missed you.

> *"Yed."*

This is who I said should be played by Ryan Reynolds.

> *"I never agreed to this! Why would you do that to me? Can't I be played by Jim Carrey? Well, the Jim Carrey from Ace Ventura anyway. Don't I get a say in the matter?"*

You'll see him say things every now and then. I won't always respond to him, but I will try to keep his input relevant to the conversation at hand.

The reason I'm even letting him have a voice at all in this book is to help demonstrate what I am genuinely feeling and thinking as I write.

> *"You can't force me to talk! Where are my royalties? What if I decide to lie about your feelings and thoughts? Then you're fucked! Now let's talk about those royalties!"*

Sigh.

I will be letting his voice through to show you how my depression and anxieties manifest in my thoughts. I want you to see those thoughts and to show you that even though we're individuals, we're not all that different. How my mind works as someone who lives with depression is not significantly different from someone else's mind who lives with anxiety, or even someone else's mind who has no diagnosed condition.

I hope it shows that mental health and wellbeing is important to all of us.

I really hope this doesn't backfire.

> *"It's already backfired. They think you're crazy. Multiple personalities! They're only continuing to read to watch the car crash. I'm driving us straight off the cliff, Thelma; I'm not even going to ask if you're certain that you want to keep going!"*

What you'll see, or hopefully will see, is all the different aspects of my inner monologue.

He's a dick.

> *"Fuck you."*

He's constantly insulting me.

> *"You shit bastard."*

He makes me feel unwelcome in my own body.

> *"Stop trying to be so nice. It's not who you really are!"*

But he cares for me.

> *"Wait, what?"*

He wants me to achieve my potential.

"You're better than this."

He protects me from harm.

"You need to stand up for yourself."

We argue. We fight. We contradict one another. But at the end of the day, we are a unit.

"Suck my unit."

We care for one another in our own special way. It's only recently in my life that I really started accepting him for who he is. He's always been there; I just didn't want to listen to him. He has been warning me about decisions I've been making for years and I only have myself to blame for the consequences.

"Told you so!"

Hopefully through hearing my inner monologue talk alongside my actual voice, you will see how living with depression is no different to how others live without it. Knowing I have depression and having spent time getting to know my inner monologue, I consider myself much happier and a lot more grounded than when I tried to keep him quiet and unheard.

My inner monologue will talk both about the past and about the present. He will refer to what I was saying to myself in the past through a retrospective view but will also refer to what I am saying and feeling as I write this book and recount all my past mistakes and failures.

What you should remember though, is that regardless of how negative he can come across at times, I like him. Before I was ashamed of talking to myself; now I embrace it. Getting comfortable and happy with yourself is one of the best things you can do for self-development and a lot of this book will build on this philosophy.

So, there you have it: I'll be telling my story and won't give a shit whether you understand the jokes I'm making or not.

> *"They'll understand them. They're just not funny."*

This is how my mind works. Hopefully it will give you insight into what a mind with depression can be like. If not, it'll be a complete cluster-fuck of embarrassment and shame that'll haunt me for a lifetime, but it should at least be funny to watch.

Either way, you win.

Right?

> *"Right."*

TWO

SPOON THEORY AND THERMODYNAMICS

Spoon Theory

IDEA

This chapter, much like this paragraph, is one of scene setting.

"It's so meta even this acronym."

It will hopefully provide you with some insight into the tools I use and consider in my life. They're not going to change your world overnight. It took me decades to appreciate them fully. They will just provide a little bit of context. Almost all these tools relate to how you manage and look after yourself with regards to your energy and your time. Hopefully you will find them useful!

Whilst at university, my ex-wife, then girlfriend, struggled with chronic fatigue syndrome. There was, and still is, very little known about it. Some believe it is a physical ailment, some believe it is a mental ailment. The research isn't conclusive either way.

I knew nothing.

"Jon Snow."

All I wanted was to care for her and help her; maybe help her recover from it, but regardless to help her live a happy life.

She found an article on spoon theory.[3]

I laughed.

---

[3] https://butyoudontlooksick.com/articles/written-by-christine/the-spoon-theory/ Accessed on 30/08/19

"The fuck is this bullshit. It sounds so ridiculous."

I listened.

Spoon theory is a simple idea that basically states that everything you do in life costs a set number of spoons determined by the amount of energy required to do it.

"Teaspoons? Tablespoons? Soup spoons? Wooden spoons?"

This energy could be physical energy, such as carrying the shopping in from the car. It could be mental energy, like doing your assignments for the week. It could even be emotional energy, like that spent grieving or celebrating. Everything costs spoons.

So far, so simple.

It goes on to say that small differences in tasks can result in large differences in spoon costs. For example, having a shower might cost two spoons; however, having a shower and washing your hair might cost five spoons because your arms need to be lifted over your head and you need to spend the time cleaning your hair. Longer hair requires even more spoons!

Slowly but surely you continue to spend spoons throughout the day doing whatever it is you need to do. Let's say for simplicity's sake that we have fifty spoons for a day. The article went on to say that people with chronic fatigue have a smaller spoon allotment each day, say thirty.

It all began to make sense.

"Did it? I still don't understand why spoons are necessary."

Expanding upon the basics, if you were feeling adventurous, you could borrow spoons from tomorrow. We all have those days where we just want to have fun and say that 'we'll pay for it tomorrow'. This is just another way of interpreting it.

Similarly, we could save up some spoons. Sadly, spoons waste after time when unused so only a small amount can carry over.

We learned to balance our spoons and slowly but surely my ex-wife began to take control of her life again.

Take a step back for a second and think of how it was for us as a couple. I could spend eighty spoons in a day doing something exciting and wonderful. I would regret it tomorrow as I stole thirty spoons, leaving me with only twenty to get through the next day. Maybe I would then borrow twenty for the day after and get through on forty spoons. The next day I would have thirty spoons, maybe borrow ten from the day after, leaving me with forty.

"Holy fuck! You're describing a hangover with spoons."

If my ex-wife were to do the same, with her reduced daily number of spoons, she'd already have spent almost three days' worth of spoons on the first day, which could completely write off the next few days and it could potentially take her up to a week to recover.

Spoons became very important in our relationship.

Not only were we responsible for our own spoons, but we also became responsible for our partner's spoons.

Spoons became our life for a time.

DEBT

Spoons are hard to relate to though.

"Finally!"

Let's look at this from a professional perspective. What if rather than a person we were looking at a company? And rather than looking at spoons, we were considering cash flow and cash flow versus budget?

We have a monthly budget of fifty that we need to achieve to meet our covenant requirements. If we breach our covenant requirements, we lose our company. It's game over.

"Game over, man. Game over."

We've had a bad month for cash flow and we only made forty-five. It's bad. How do we get out of this?

I do not advocate any of this next part, but I can assure you I have witnessed this and worse within various organisations. To any auditors reading this, when you're looking at the results by month, ask to see what date the ledgers closed. You'll be in for a surprise!

How about we leave the ledger open a little bit and capture some cash flow from the next month? Shouldn't be too bad, right? We can recoup it by pushing a little bit harder next month. We decide to leave the ledger open and reach our budgeted figure of fifty for the month.

Where's the problem here?

We've immediately started our next month at negative five.

Our budget could be seen to have increased to fifty-five for the next month. We need to work harder to simply stand still. What if this continues? Maybe we need to pull ten forwards next month, then fifteen the month after and before long we're reliant on future sales and cash flow to survive.

If this was the situation with one of your clients, what would you recommend? There are lots of options available here objectively speaking, but most involve some form of refinancing.

It's become apparent that there is a now a constant level of debt in the business, so rather than managing it with expensive short-term loans such as invoice financing, asset-based lending and the like, let's convert it all to long-term debt and make it more regular and easier to manage.

Step back into the real world with people and their spoons.

"Did you really just say that?"

How do you refinance your spoons? You're constantly spending the spoons of tomorrow today. Where do you go to seek a lending provider? How do you convert the short-term spoon debt into long-term spoon debt? How do you survive this strain on your spoons?

This is a breakdown.

This is your warning sign.

Stop.

Stop now!

You can't refinance your spoons without stopping. You can't stop going without a break from your heavy spoon-spending habits.

Now what if I posited that your daily spoon allowance would decrease every year from your twenty-first birthday until the day you die? Every year, every month, every week, every day slightly fewer spoons to spend. You still must do everything the same, just with fewer and fewer spoons. Maybe it doesn't start at twenty-one. Maybe you get to hold onto a spoon for a little bit without it decaying. Slowly but surely though, time will take them all away from you. In the end, when you have no spoons left to spend, you die and slowly fade into the entropic spoon-less void.

> *"You are fucking bleak dude. Lighten up."*

This is growing old.

> *"No. This is a horrific image you've just traumatised the readers with! I'm not sure I want to be part of this anymore. Can I get off this ride?"*

It took me a long time to fully understand the depth of spoon theory and how relevant it is to all life; not just those suffering with a chronic condition. Spoon theory allows me to know when I need a break or know that I will need to rest before I do something else.

RULE

With spoon theory as an aid we can see where the limitations in our lives come from. Not only do we have a finite lifetime, but we also have finite spoons.

Life is about balancing spoons.

> *"Please, don't let this be the quote we're remembered for. Fuck. Why am I cursed to talk in these italics? I just want to scribble that out so there's no way it can be remembered at all. Life is about balancing spoons. Fuck's sake."*

We balance our spoons to make sure we can do what we want to do whilst we have the spoons remaining to do it. As our spoons diminish over time, we can't do the things we used to be able to do.

When we're young and at university we can drink to excess almost daily with little to no consequences and can immediately get back on it the next day. As an adult though we can barely stay awake after one or two drinks, need our early bedtime and can feel the hangover for the next few days.

> *"Fuck being an adult. Living life as an adult is like folding a fitted sheet!"*

Knowing that there is a need to balance spoons allows us to plan our spoon-spending habits accordingly. Knowing you have a big weekend coming up, take a break ahead of time or plan some time off afterwards. If you're able to do so, try and save some spoons in advance so you're not borrowing from your future. The reason for this is that – just like in finance – where you can have a spoon debt, you can also have a spoon asset.

If you're going out on a Saturday for a big event that you know will be draining and could eat into your Sunday and maybe even Monday, rest on the Friday night ahead of time and don't plan anything for the Sunday other than to recover.

Just like in finance though, spoon assets depreciate over time and spoon debt collects compound interest. Managing these is incredibly important to bringing real balance and energy back into your life.

Everything in moderation. Even spoons.

Thinking with spoons initially sounds quite boring and dull. It feels like you're constraining and limiting what you can do and what you can enjoy. You'll feel fine and want to keep going. The important part is to begin listening to yourself. You have a wealth of experience from the years you've been alive. Look back. Are there times when you were full of energy, went to do something and then just felt worse as a result? This could be because you've spent some extra spoons without realising it. Maybe you were out for a leaving do with work spending physical spoons, but there were a lot of emotional spoons spent because you didn't want to see your colleague leave and so felt drained the next day.

Spoon theory is here to help you understand what's going on with your body.

The Conservation of Energy

BUZZ

I never thought I'd be writing about thermodynamics. I thought my days of writing about physics were done. It's nice to use my degree for a change!

> *"Yeah, about that. Four years and not used any of it even once in your career."*

Quiet you!

The First Law of Thermodynamics[4] is often referred to as 'The Law of Conservation of Energy' and simply states that energy cannot be created or destroyed, only transferred or exchanged. Our bodies consume food and in exchange convert the chemical potential energy in the sugars and other foodstuffs into kinetic energy as we walk, electrical energy as we think and different chemical potential energies to store for later use. It's a beautifully complex process that we never really need to worry about in our daily lives. We put food in, we get to do stuff.

Simple.

Where this comes undone is when we struggle to look after our bodies. Maybe we overuse them, maybe we damage them, maybe the food we consume isn't easy to convert to the right energy we need, maybe we're just getting older. However it happens, we find ourselves with less energy than we did previously.

---

[4] *Thermodynamics. An Advanced Treatment for Chemists and Physicists*, seventh edition. Amsterdam: North-Holland

We find ourselves with fewer spoons.

"Not again."

ROOT

Spoons do not grow on trees.

Spoons are not handed out at the beginning or end of a day. Spoons are not instantly attained through some mysterious arcane art or can of coconut Red Bull! You may get some temporary spoons from that can, but all that does is create a larger deficit that needs repaying in the future.

Spoons come from rest. Spoons come from sleep. Spoons come from relaxation.

The problem here is that rest for one person isn't necessarily rest for another and it's important to rest in a way appropriate to you.

We are all different and beautifully unique, but for simplicity of explanation let's put us all in sixteen pigeonholes and put some labels on us.

"Kind of like what society does to us all the time."

Myers-Briggs[5] is a well-known personality type indicator. It is well documented with lots of information accessible online or in books. I am not going into the detail of it here, but essentially it categorises personalities into sixteen different tropes based on four axes. These are

---

[5] *Gifts Differing: Understanding Personality Type*. Mountain View, CA: Davies-Black Publishing

Introversion/Extroversion, Sensing/Intuition, Thinking/ Feeling and Judging/Perceiving.

In every test I have ever done at every stage in my life and career, my personality type always falls as an ENTJ.[6] This means I am an extrovert who prefers taking in information intuitively, making decisions through thinking and interacting with others through judgement. This puts me in the 'Commander' category, which is summarised as a bold and imaginative leader who will always find a way and if not will make one.

> *"You absolutely love saying that about yourself. You try your hardest to make it sound bad but underneath it all you absolutely love it!"*

Looking closer at my results, my Introversion/ Extroversion score was only slightly in the Extrovert category. When looking further into this I began to see that the definition of Introversion/Extroversion was not what I originally thought. I was assuming this was about how you interacted outwardly. People who are loud and somewhat obnoxious are often called extroverts. People who are quiet and shy are often called introverts. The definition used was something completely different. It was about how you rest. It was about where your energy comes from. It was about your source of spoons.

For me, I knew I was an extrovert, so where did my spoons come from? Extroverts typically recover spoons from social interaction where they can be outgoing. I finally

---

[6] www.16personalities.com/personality-types Accessed on 30/08/19

understood a bit more about myself. I always struggled with long days in an office and went home feeling exhausted. I was sedentary, so I wasn't spending energy, so why was I so tired? It was because I wasn't recovering my energy, my spoons, through any meaningful interactions with people. It also explained why, when I was having quiet weekends not doing anything, I often felt a bit stir crazy and wanted to go back to work on Monday.

"Mondays are the absolute worst!

But what I also found after trying to recover spoons through my extroversion was that I needed introversion as well. It makes sense when you think about the results of the Myers-Briggs test. There were times when all I wanted to do was sit and think, or get lost in a video game, maybe do something creative. I suddenly found that this balance was necessary for me to be able to feel properly rested.

Why is this important to you then?

Professional life, in fact just life in general, comes with many pressures. Balancing your spoons and managing your energy will be important for you to be able to do everything you want whilst you have the spoons to be able to do it. Getting to know yourself and your body is incredibly important. You need to learn how you rest and what brings you the happiness that comes with good rest. There are lots of 'get healthy quick' schemes out there, lots of 'alternative medicines' and lots of ways to do things. Not all of them will work for you. You're an individual, you will need to figure out which do and which don't.

I know that I need to balance the introversion and extroversion in my life. I always make sure to have at least one social engagement planned during a week, whether it is going out for drinks with work, seeing friends or just a busy day of meetings with new people. I also always make sure I have time to myself to reflect on things. I make sure to keep certain evenings free, or weekend days to just do jobs and chores around the house. Sometimes I'll have nothing planned and just sit quietly. I hate it, but I know it helps me. I also know that music plays a large part in where my energy comes from and has a big impact on my mood, so I always make sure to listen to music when I can. Exploring myself and what makes a difference to my life and my happiness has played a large part in my acceptance of living with depression. Understanding me makes living alone easier as it's no longer about filling the void of time between things; it has become about getting to know myself more or getting better acquainted with my inner critic.

I know that when I am struggling with my inner critic,

> *"Hey again, did you think I'd gone away? I was just taking a break and letting you monologue for a bit. Needed to save my spoons and all…"*

or feeling low on energy, or just having a bad day where nothing seems to be going right I should focus on the things that bring me happiness, increase my energy and make me feel better. I put on music, I speak to someone and I take myself out of the situation I'm in. Obviously, we have obligations that we are required to do in life, whether for work, for ourselves, for our home or for others. We need to do what we need to do. Outside of that, however, think about what you need and what you want!

Learn to be selfish.

One Fine Day

PART

Time is finite.

Whatever you have learned, whatever physics teaches us, there is one undeniable fact: eventually you will die.

> *"Soon. Please, soon. Just anything to stop being a part of this stupid book."*

Many extend this to: you will die, and you will get taxed whilst you live.

Death and taxes after all.

Death and taxes.

It's why we accountants and lawyers exist. We exist to mitigate tax and organise the payment of tax whilst doing so in accordance with the laws of our world. We try to put pretty names on it, but fundamentally, we survive on people's success and failure.

> *"Ouch."*

Knowing death is coming isn't a bad thing though. It means we know eventually our time will end, but until it happens, we can live and can enjoy our lives. Many people crave experiences and relentlessly post about them on social media. Those people want to show you that they have done something they consider valuable during their fleeting time.

Sickening in a way when you think about it. They want you to spend some of your finite time looking at pictures of them spending some of their finite time in a far more exciting way than looking at pictures of their excitement.

Let us take the natural extension of this and look at how a single day is finite. We have twenty-four hours a day to do what we want and need. We can't steal time from tomorrow as we stole spoons previously. We have a finite boundary condition here and it is very real.

"No one cares about discrete mathematics!"

How do we spend a typical day? What does a normal day look like? We'll ignore weekends as those vary too much. Let's look at a normal working day.

On average we sleep approximately eight hours a night. This will vary depending on each individual, but broadly speaking somewhere around eight hours of consistent sleep is good for us.

"You haven't had a proper good night of sleep in a decade or two."

According to the Office for National Statistics,[7] a typical workday across all industries involves eight hours of our time as well, combined with a commute of approximately thirty minutes each way.

---

[7] www.ons.gov.uk/employmentandlabourmarket/peopleinwork Accessed on 30/08/19

So out of our initial twenty-four hours, seventeen of them are already committed. This leaves us with seven.

"Over two thirds gone already. I don't really want to be doing either of these!"

Statistics show we spend roughly two hours preparing food and eating food throughout a day. Again, not unreasonable with approximately thirty minutes a meal and then a bit more for preparation and so on. We also spend roughly two hours on hygiene and cleanliness, including having a shower or a bath, brushing our teeth, going to the toilet and then all the cleaning following such activities and the wider household. Here's another four hours dedicated to simply existing in a clean household.

"This deal is getting worse all the time."

Well, I'm altering the deal; pray that I don't alter it any further.

We now have three hours left in our day. This sounds ridiculous, right? Three hours left to do stuff we want to do. Well, we haven't included communicating with or caring for others yet. Whether it be children, pets or relatives, we spend almost an hour each day looking after someone. This could be feeding your cats or putting your children to bed or even getting them up and ready for school. The point is, it is adding up and fast!

Finally, we have exercise and other health-related activities such as sports. On average almost an hour each day is spent on maintaining your health.

Now remember, this is an average day. You may not exercise or care for others every day, so some of that time is freed up, but then on days when you are doing it, it may take more time etc.

We have all this time already committed to looking after ourselves, our homes, our families and our work. What time do we have left to do things we enjoy? What is left for us?

One hour.

One fucking hour.

Sixty minutes to do what you want to do.

Better make it count!

Obviously, these are only statistical averages across huge and varied sample sizes; but there's only one hour a day to do what you want. It's easy to see why people 'live for the weekend'; at least on weekends you can spend more time on yourself and doing what you want.

> *"Do you though? How much of the time do you actually do what you want?"*

It's scary when you look at it like this.

I now feel a little bit anxious about making sure that one hour counts for something. Even worse I feel even more anxious about the days when I spent hours on an evening in front of a computer ignoring all those other important things in life. Did I really manage to get away with neglecting all those other parts of my life?

> *"No. Your life has an almost end. That neglect caught up to you and almost killed you."*

We are the only ones who truly have control over how our time is spent each day.

Let's make sure that it's put to good use.

DROP

Knowing what a typical day looks like doesn't change how we respond to changes in our typical day though. Just as with our spoon requirements for each day, there will be different time requirements each day. Sometimes we may need to work extra time because we have a deadline that needs to be met. Sometimes it may be that a child is sick and needs collecting from school and then looking after when we get home. Life happens. It just does.

Luckily, things are getting easier.

Technology is great. It allows us to work from home and multitask some of these activities. Our employers are great. They understand we have other commitments and let us manage our time and trust us accordingly. We live in a great age where we have the utmost control over our lives.

But what happens when we can't? What happens when we must work from the office? Or maybe we perceive that we should be based in the office even if it's not necessary. What happens if we just can't multitask and need to commit the extra time?

We make sacrifices.

Just as life is a balancing act of spoons and time, it's also a balancing act of responsibilities. We become experts in keeping plates spinning. Every day another set of spinning plates needs keeping in check. Every night we pray that when we go to sleep the plates won't fall. Every morning we wake up and make sure to keep them spinning again. But eventually there's one too many plates. Sacrifices must be made to keep the other plates spinning. Which of our plates is the first to fall?

"Enough with the rhetorical questions."

Our personal time and our sleep are the first sacrifices we make.

Without a single thought, if we're asked to work late and get something done, we'll do it. We'll work longer and harder, choosing to 'not go play squash tonight' or 'not have that piano lesson'. We may have even paid in advance for the game or lesson and we choose to forgo our own money by cancelling, but that's okay, we're doing this for the greater good, we'll be rewarded in kind.

"In due course of course."

This is okay to begin with. It's just like borrowing spoons from tomorrow. You can sacrifice a bit here or there. You can give up on some of the things you care about for now. You can make it up at the weekend. It'll be okay.

Will it?

"It never is."

What happens if something urgent comes in on Friday and you're needed to drop all your plans for the weekend and work instead? What happens if the constant borrowing of time completely removes your ability to do what you want to do?

Just like with our spoon debt we end up with a time debt, or at the very least an enjoyment debt. Eventually that debt needs repaying.

This is burnout.

This is when we break.

YOUR

You must learn to keep your 'you time'.

Your time is yours and yours alone.

You choose what to do with it.

You are welcome to give it to others but know that is your decision! And make it a conscious decision rather than just a default one!

During a therapy session one day I was introduced to the concept of Your Ship.

I laughed.

"Ha!"

You draw a ship. You divide it into sections based on what your life is like. I believe you're told to do it based on how much time you spend thinking about each subject, but it doesn't matter if you do it based on time spent or some other metric, it's conceptual after all.

The purpose of the exercise is to see how your 'cargo' and 'freight' are balanced. Are you heavily weighted towards work? You'll probably sink. Are you over-encumbered with your children? You'll probably sink. Are you spending too much time worrying about nothing? You'll probably sink.

The idea is that by drawing it out on paper, you are forced to visualise the, often many, imbalances in your life. Often we can't see them whilst we're living with them, so this forces you to see them.

There's a quote from somewhere, I have no idea where. I can't even find who said it on Google which probably means it's either ancient wisdom that transcends time or it's absolute rubbish. Whichever it is, when I heard it, it meant something to me.

The saying simply goes: 'Why spend eight hours a day working for someone on their dreams and ambitions and then come home and not work on your own dreams and ambitions?'

> *"Spending eight hours a day would be a fucking luxury. More like spending eleven hours a day, some of your evenings and half your weekend."*

Every time I made a concession for work, every time I gave up a weekend, every time I was thinking about work rather than enjoying the moment I was living in I was slowly but surely giving up on my dreams and ambitions. I heard this saying and I looked back on my life, realising just how imbalanced My Ship really was. I was sad. I was remorseful. I was angry. My dreams, my ambitions, my wants and my hopes were left by the wayside as I pursued a career that I ultimately felt no love for. I made the choices because it felt like it was expected of me.

> *"You never listened."*

We all do it.

We all know we do it.

Do you have the courage to change it?

Do you have the strength to keep hold of your dreams and ambitions?

The Hero of Time

NOPE

You are your own hero.

This is your heroic journey after all.

You have absolute power and control over your spoons and your time. You can make your own decisions, despite how helpless you may feel at times. Work is demanding. Life is demanding. Only you can choose what is right for you.

The most important thing I ever learned in life was that I could say no.

"No."

It was a revelation.

"No. Not really."

What was stranger than the realisation I could say no was the strength that came with it! I felt I had control again. I felt in control for the first time in a long time.

"The illusion of free will is not free will."

I was working with a client. I was working with them on their business change strategy and how to position them better for growth in the future. It was fun. I love projects like this as it brings an entire business together. I was one of only two qualified accountants working in the business apart from the Finance Director. The second was going on maternity leave and the business would need an interim to cover her.

"Fuck no."

I knew it was coming. I knew it was going to happen. I knew the signs when I saw them. I know how Finance Directors work. I was going to be asked to be the interim and be the Financial Controller for the business.

This was a nightmare for me. I knew from previous experience this sort of role wasn't for me. Far too much day-to-day and not enough excitement and interest to keep me entertained. I knew I would have to say no. But saying no was terrifying. They could potentially force me into the role, make my change-focused position redundant yet offer me this as an alternative so they could be doing the right thing.

I was stuck.

It was going to be a fight for my wellbeing.

Can you really put your own happiness first in this situation? I'd never even considered it. I knew I would be miserable. It would likely lead to a repeat of one of my previous periods of deep depression and unhappiness. My heart was pounding. My head was spinning. It was painful thinking through this decision. 'What if you did the interim Financial Controller role for the maternity cover, Andy? You're more than qualified, it'd only be for a year and you'd get to know the business so well. It'd also save us money which is also great.'

"ARGH!"

No.

I was doing it.

"I'm proud of you. Or me? Proud of us."

No. I am not really interested in being a Financial Controller. It's just not something I'm interested in. I enjoy the work I do with change and strategy too much. I don't want to lose that enjoyment from my work.

But.

"Why add anything else?"

I will help you find the right interim. I'll make sure they do a better job than I would do. You'll get your Financial Controller. Just like that, I had stood up for myself. Not only did I stand up for what I believed in, I positioned myself much better for the future. I had shown that I wasn't the sort of person to be pushed around. I was willing to stand my ground. The respect I gained from that one word, both from colleagues and from myself, was worth all the fear and stress that came before it.

Nowadays, I say no an awful lot more.

I have turned down work. I have turned down clients. I have left positions. I have said no a lot more than I probably should if I'm honest!

I am standing up for myself. I am standing up for my beliefs. I am standing up for my moral compass. I am happier than I ever have been before because I am now taking control of my time. No is such a simple word. It may even be one of the first we learn.

"It was your youngest brother's first word."

Start saying no and taking control.

MINE

Unfortunately, we can't always say no though.

It's ridiculous, isn't it? I tell you that you should be saying no and then immediately take the ability away from you.

"It's just like the beginning of every Metroid game!"

Sometimes, you just need to put the hours in and do the work. It sucks. I know. I have put in countless hours doing work above and beyond what is expected. I have worked every hour in the day. It is painful. It is tough. Sometimes though, it just needs to be done.

So how do you manage this situation? How do you save yourself without saying no? How can you protect your spoons and time as best as possible?

Again, you already know the answer. It's not a secret. You take the time back you are owed. Some employers have formal Time Owed in Lieu policies that cover staff and allow them to recoup additional hours worked. Other employers may have Over Time rules that help people earn extra for working above and beyond what they are contracted to do, perhaps with a limit to protect from people trying to abuse the system. Some employers ask you to waive all rights to the maximum hours part of the employment regulations[8] so that you have no protection, simply saying that you will work whatever time is necessary to complete the task at hand.

"That last one doesn't sound that great."

Did you read your contract? Where are you on this scale?

"Let's be honest here. If you are ever referring to your contract when speaking to your employer, you're probably not going to be working there much longer anyway."

Regardless of what you are contractually obliged to, you need to look after yourself. You need to make sure you can do the extra hours again should they be required again. So how?

Take what is yours. Take your time back.

Easier said than done I know.

Presenteeism is a real issue. We feel we should be at work because that is what we believe is expected of us. We go into the office, or to school, even when we are sick just to show how dedicated we are. We then get sent home with two to three hours of potential rest wasted trying to look like a committed employee. This isn't just the case with physical illnesses though. Presenteeism represents two thirds of all time lost in the UK. You'd think it'd be absenteeism, but it's the other way around. Those times when you're sat in the office worried about a loved

---

[8] www.gov.uk/maximum-weekly-working-hours Accessed on 30/08/19

one. Those times when you're heartbroken and can't concentrate. Those times when you have a million and one other things on your mind. You sit in the office and are almost paralysed with thoughts in your head. You never get any work done in these situations, so why try?

If you are not needed in the office, ask to work from home. If you are in the position where you can make that decision, choose to work from home!

If you don't have a reason to stay late, get out of the office early and beat the traffic. You may not recover all the extra time you have worked, but you will get a little bit back. As harsh as it sounds, you are the only person who will fight for your time, so if you're not protecting yourself then you're vulnerable to everything the world could demand from you.

ROSE

With our busy lives and the demands placed on ourselves from work, friends, family and all the rest, it can be hard to get time to ourselves. Life is busy and responsibilities are many, but that doesn't mean we can't stop occasionally.

"The guilt will set in as soon as you do."

I remember in the days leading up to my wedding to my now ex-wife, people were saying so many things to me, it was hard to take anything in. One person said something to me that stood out. I can't remember who it was, but thank you. I have passed on these words to all my friends who have married since then and they have all appreciated every word.

Take some time together for just the two of you. It is your wedding day. Make memories together.

Fairly simple, isn't it? Makes loads of sense. The issue is that a wedding nowadays is an event. Everyone loves a party, and everyone has come to celebrate you. They'll all want to speak to you and it's incredibly easy to get dragged along with the crowd.

There were two moments I will remember forever. Despite all the heart ache and pain that followed, these are moments that meant something to me.

Firstly, there was a moment when the guests were being seated for the wedding breakfast. We stood together alone in a field listening to a string quartet play a song we had requested. It was peaceful. It was special. It meant something to us. The second is one about midway through the afternoon. People were busy enjoying themselves in the sun and I escaped by myself and just sat. I sat alone. I kept quiet. I listened. I felt what was around me. It allowed me to ground myself from all the chaos and celebration in the atmosphere.

One is a memory of creating something together. We chose that song. We chose that moment. It was just us. The other is a memory of tranquillity and satisfaction. I had just got married. I had made a then-lifelong commitment to someone. I was at peace with the world.

It's easy to get swallowed up in what's going on around you. It's easy to lose track of where you've been and where you're going. The tides of time never stop and there is a constant feeling of pressure that we must be doing something that moves us in the direction of success and progression.

It's hard to stop.

I know.

I never stopped and then I almost stopped everything.

When you do get a chance to stop. Breathe. Relax. Take it in. We hear all the time about how we should stop and smell the roses. It's so important to do so. Everything around us can be so distracting and the journey never seems to end. When there is a break in the excitement, or a calm before a storm, do take a break. Doing nothing isn't nothing, it's choosing to not do something!

Enjoy it. You have earned it.

> *"No, you haven't. There's so much more to do."*

You have earned it! Despite what your inner critic may tell you. Enjoy it.

One Mind, One Body, One Cup

TOIL

We only have one mind and one body. I am trying to explain how neglecting to care for your mind can have extremely serious consequences, but it would be remiss of me to not talk somewhere about your body. The mind and body are linked. Neither can live without the other. You must take care of them both together.

> *"You shouldn't talk about your body. You don't look after yourself. You're overweight, don't exercise and are unattractive."*

Work impacts our body in many subtle and sometimes not-so-subtle ways.

If you are an office-based worker, the biggest issue you will have is that you are sedentary for most of the day. We sit at laptops typing away, hunched backs, crooked necks, repeatedly tapping with our fingers, staring at screens burning our retinas with artificial light. The human body didn't evolve as it has, to do this for eight to ten hours a day!

This is not a good start.

There are many tried and true methods of answering all these issues. There are entire departments and functions dedicated to your physical wellbeing whilst working because companies and organisations do understand the damage this can cause to your bodies; mostly because they want you to be a good little worker bee!

The way I combatted a lot of these issues was simply by not sitting down. I stopped e-mailing people in the same building. I stood up, walked to their desk, had a conversation, walked back. Not only does this help with your physical wellbeing by getting at the very least some minor exercise in, it also helps with your mental wellbeing by giving you a meaningful interaction with another person. I forced myself to do this at least once a day to begin with and I felt better because of it. I also always tried to go for a walk at lunch time. It didn't need to be to go buy lunch or anything, it just needed to be enough to stand outside in the fresh air and to ever so slightly get my heart beating.

It's not much, but small changes do add up and can do a lot over the course of a lifetime!

One of the best things I ever did in my life was moving closer to where I worked. Commuting is draining. You wake up early, get ready in a rush, just about pull your head together enough to think you're able to start working and then sit in a car or on a bus for thirty minutes. You lose all momentum when commuting for a long time. When I moved closer to work, I started walking to work. This helped me in a couple of ways. Firstly, I didn't lose momentum from commuting. I got up as usual, but then a thirty minute to an hour walk each morning got my body and brain active. I was able to enter the office and start working as soon as I sat down.

"Well. Don't forget the coffee!"

Secondly though, I hate going to the gym. I hate the idea of losing what precious free time I have doing something I don't enjoy. However, I love efficiency. There's nothing more efficient than combining two tasks into one, doubling your output in the same time, or halving the total time spent. This is what project managers dream of – well, this and Gantt charts.

By being able to walk to work, I was able to include exercise in my daily routine whilst keeping my time at home to myself. This isn't practical for everyone, but if you can find a way to bring exercise into your life in a meaningful way outside of just going to the gym then you will feel better because of it.

As you can see, I am lazy. I am fundamentally lazy. I just want to be at home with my cat, chilling out and enjoying my time doing what I want to do.

"Or being at the pub and watching the world go by."

Anyone who says they're not lazy is lying to themselves. They'll say things like 'I live to work' or 'I'd get bored without work'. Believe me, I've said them enough! Knowing I'm lazy pushes me towards efficiency and making small improvements where I can. If I can automate something, or save time in a process, I will. I enjoy programming and scripting as it allows me to combine multiple things into one, releasing more time back to me. Some people hate this. Some people like putting in the hours and the elbow grease to get things done. I'm just not one of them. In my work I push to automate everything and make myself redundant.

That's when I know my work is done!

"It's also probably why you've ended up writing a book."

Whilst this book will continue to focus on the mental aspects of wellbeing, remember that the mind and the body are inherently linked. You cannot fix a mind with a broken body and cannot fix a body with a broken mind.

PUSH

Now to complicate things a bit further. Your mental health can have direct physical consequences on your body and it's not good. Just as we talked about previously where a healthier body can help you have a healthier mind, the reverse is true.

It's easy to forget this on our busy journey. I know I did.

Whilst I was coming towards the end of my training contract as an accountant, I found myself under a lot of stress. It's probably no different than an average amount of stress in a normal working life, but it felt like a lot at the time. This included stress from exams and the workload required to pass first time, the deadlines for various projects and proposals I needed to deliver and then everything else that goes on in life that requires thought and attention. I found myself getting more and more tired each day that it carried on. I was exhausted. My spoons were diminishing.

"Sounds familiar."

Then something happened. I noticed I was going to the toilet a lot more often, specifically right before bed. Then about five minutes after I got into bed, I needed to go again. Then maybe ten minutes after that, again. I just kept needing to go to the bathroom. Each time I sat there contemplating why I still needed the toilet. I started worrying about not being able to make it to the bathroom in time and 'having an accident' during the night. How embarrassing would that be! Especially whilst sharing the bed with someone! I was so concerned about it I started sleeping with a pillow over my crotch in the hope of catching anything before it was noticed. Luckily it was never necessary, but I was so scared of the embarrassment of it happening I had to do something. It was awful. This carried on for a good few months.

Eventually, my now ex-wife convinced me to go to see a doctor about it. I was embarrassed beyond belief.

It was the first question that got me the most though. Immediately after I explained what the issue was, I was asked a very simple and very awkward question: 'Do you want me to look?'

"No, I don't want you to fucking look. Stay the fuck away."

After much embarrassment and awkwardness, we concluded that this was all stress related. Stress, which is something I always thought was limited to the mind, had now started affecting my body. I knew I was mentally fatigued due to stress. I knew I was tired and was pushing myself too hard with work. I just had no idea it could have such an impact on my body. I mean, my body wasn't and probably still isn't in a great shape, but this just made everything worse.

I needed to address the mental to start restoring balance to the physical. It took me a while to do so and is something that I still work on to this day. It isn't always easy to notice how these things are connected. Sometimes you do need to stop, pause and review where you are and what is going on.

Your mind matters! Don't let it ever reach a stage where it starts making your body suffer to get noticed!

FOOD

I love food.

"That's because you're fat."

That's why I'm fat.

"Touché!"

I love everything about food. I love cooking. I love tasting. I love eating. I love sharing. Food is just brilliant. I will gladly cook a two or three course meal from scratch every night after a long day at work just because of the pleasure it brings me. I find real joy in the preparation of food alongside someone else. It's sharing in creativity and creating something to enjoy and share together.

My love of food has always led me to be slightly overweight.

"Slightly?"

Now because I love food, food comforts me. Food makes me feel better. Food also distracts me. If I'm having a bad day, feeling down, feeling like the world has turned against me, whatever, I comfort myself with food. I will either cook or order in something that probably has way more than my daily allowance of calories. It's great. I'm suddenly feeling much better as I've enjoyed something that brings me genuine happiness. The problem is that this feeling is fleeting. Within a few hours, I'll almost certainly feel bad again, except now I'm also feeling guilty for eating far too much. A vicious cycle ensues!

We mentioned previously that the first things we sacrifice when our time is pressured are our free time and our sleep. The next on the chopping block is often our food and food preparation. Again, modern convenience to save the day. We can now get food delivered to us from a restaurant!

We can eat a banquet of a meal whilst sat at our desk late at night working by ourselves apart from the occasional visit from a security guard to check we're not dead.

You can always see the teams where it is happening. You walk into the office and can see the pizza boxes by the bins. The sweat on their brows from exhaustion and the over-consumption of easy-to-order carbs is palpable. If you're lucky they had the opportunity to go home and shower, otherwise it is a full olfactory overload.

Even if we do manage to make it home, we're probably too tired to cook a healthy meal from scratch, so we look to takeaways or frozen ready meals. Don't get me wrong, I have great memories of fish fingers and chicken nuggets, but quickly cramming ten to twenty of them night-in night-out is not good for you.

Unfortunately, maintaining a healthy diet does matter. Whether we like it or not, our body needs the right stuff going into it. It is hard work because, again, the world wants our time and we are the only ones who will defend it.

When I was going through my separation and later divorce, I lived day-to-day. I was surviving. When you're only surviving a lot of thought goes out the window and you look for what is the easiest and quickest way to achieve what you need. For me this involved a lot of takeaway food. I ate to excess and I put on a lot of weight. I felt awful. The cycle of putting on weight, feeling worse because I was putting on weight, then comfort eating to make myself feel better and therefore putting on even more weight was never ending. I was surviving. I existed. However, it wasn't a good existence.

One day my brother told me about how he did some allergy test online. I was sceptical.

Anyway, he told me how it revealed he was gluten-intolerant and not lactose-intolerant. He had proceeded to cut gluten out of his diet and after just a week of doing this his bowels had cleared up and he was no longer gassing us at every family occasion. I thought why the hell not, it can't hurt, it's not a blood test, so it's fine.

"Your fear of needles is ridiculous at times. Have a filling without anaesthetic. Have entire sleeve of tattoos done in a year. Bit of a mixed message there!"

Six weeks later I got my results back. I was intolerant to lactose. Expected. I was intolerant to gluten. Okay, maybe it's hereditary or something. I was intolerant to garlic! Seriously, body, these are my three favourite things to cook with: cheese, bread and garlic!

The bit that was most interesting and that made me change my lifestyle was what was missing from my diet. I had a deficiency in manganese and a load of other basic nutrients and minerals. Reading into it, a deficiency in manganese can be a warning sign of diabetes. As a fat lad, I was worried!

"Fatty."

I needed to change.

It was no longer a want; it was a need.

It prompted me to make the changes that previously I had always told myself I would make tomorrow. I did the easy thing. I'm lazy after all. I ordered all my deficient nutrients in the form of supplements. I started taking almost ten different tablets a day on top of my anti-depressants and hay fever tablets. The first few days of taking these tablets, there was lightning shocking me from the inside every few minutes. It was agony. I called my mum one night from bed and I asked her to call me in the morning to make sure I wasn't dead. No joke. I was that worried.

After a week, I felt awake for the first time in months.

Clouds lifted.

I felt healthier.

I had more energy.

I had more spoons!

After seemingly losing a lot of my spoons to stress, anxiety, depression and work, surviving in a time of adversity, I had a new lease of life. I haven't gone back since.

> *"Except for when I make you feel shit. Remember, this is not a success story."*

Working on my body alone had never worked for me. Working on my mind alone just didn't work. It was only when I was approaching both in concert that I was able to make change happen.

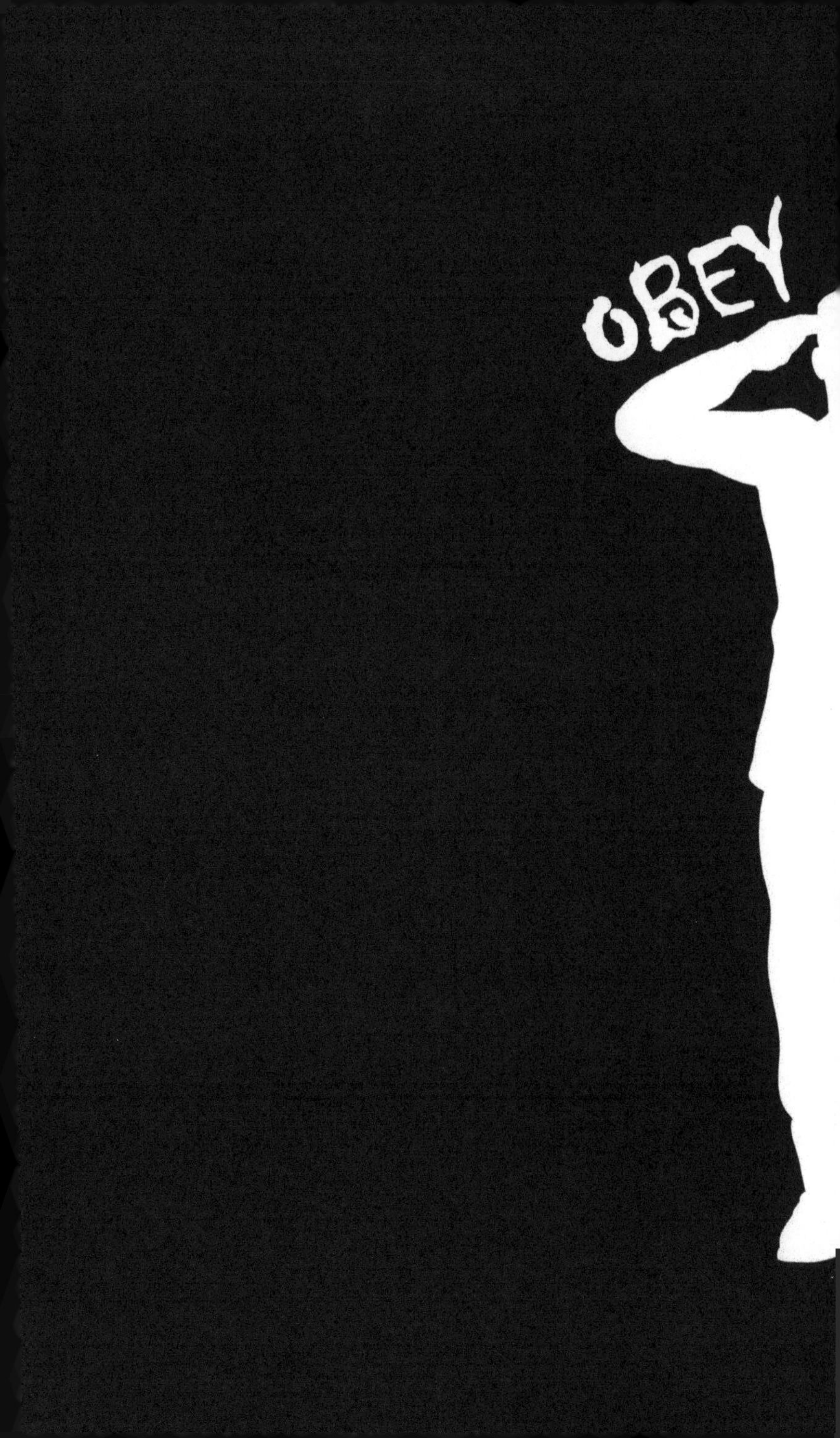
OBEY

THREE

HIGH SCHOOL NEVER ENDS

Standing Out from the In Crowd

FIRM

Bowling for Soup were right.

High School, Secondary School, whatever you want to call it, never really ends. You will be dissected by your peer group in whatever organisation you are part of, categorised into one of only a handful of pigeonholes and then that's it. That's you. At least, that's you until you move to be part of another organisation, then the process will start again.

One of the attractions of joining a professional service organisation is that it is structured very similarly to what you have experienced previously in school, college and university. You are part of a year group or intake. You will likely, but not always, be in a year group with similarly aged people. You will get promoted in the same way you moved through year groups at school. You will still go to college for some of your time during your training contract. You will be invited to numerous social events and still be able to live a similar lifestyle to the one you had at university, only this time you actually have to attend the eight hours minimum of lectures or work and will have a hell of a lot more disposable income.

"Doesn't sound bad. We were convinced pretty easily."

However, the fact that it is like school and university means it also comes with the same nuances. This chapter will talk about what life is like within a professional service firm, how it can potentially adversely impact your mental health and how you can protect yourself.

As a reminder, mostly because I'm worried everyone I have ever worked with will hate me for writing all this:

"They already hate you."

Whilst this is based on my personal experiences, your experience may be different. I do not regret any of my decisions. I have the utmost respect for all the large professional practices and just because it was not right for me doesn't mean that it isn't right for you and isn't the right way to operate in general.

POUR

The basic structure of each practice is that of a bottom-heavy funnel, leading up from Associate all the way to Partner. Legal practices have different titles for different grades, but you should get the idea: the many become the few or the one over time.

"Did you just try to quote Spock?"

Whatever is said and whatever you are told, practices are based around survival of the fittest. They are fundamentally Darwinian[9] in nature. You either succeed or die.

"There's probably some Game of Thrones reference here."

You start in a year group, say of approximately twenty to thirty people with only one of them, maybe two,

---

[9] *On the Origin of Species by Means of Natural Selection, or the Preservation of Favoured Races in the Struggle for Life.* London: John Murray

making it to Partner. This is what is expected and what needs to continue to happen for a practice to survive. The success of the partnership requires this attrition to occur, so understand that all things being equal, your odds of making it all the way to the top are slim to none!

Each Partner is their own business unit and has their own profit and loss account, using shared resource to deliver their work and grow their business. If twenty-plus people made it to Partner in one region at one time that would result in twenty-plus competing Partners all relying on the same resource, so the funnel would need to widen significantly. It would also be twenty-plus Partners each vying for work against the other Partners. As much as they say they won't compete within the firm, they do. They will also need to divide all the available work and new targets between them, resulting in much smaller earnings and profits for each Partner. It just doesn't work!

"But what about the One Firm approach?"

Why is understanding this important?

If you are committed to making it to Partner, you need to be willing and able to fight for it along the way. It is survival of the fittest. Attrition is expected. You will be competing directly against those people in your peer group and more to make it to the top of the pyramid. It can be an incredibly lonely and gruelling task, so make sure it's worth it and it's what you want.

ABLE

There is a level of confidence, maybe even arrogance, that is expected of you as you enter practice. You are the chosen one.

"Alright, Neo."

You were selected to join. Countless entered the recruitment process but you made it through. You are special. You were handpicked alongside the other twenty-odd people in your region and potentially hundreds across the country.

"I'm still the best though. Aced those psychometric entry tests. Ninety-ninth percentile and all that."

Sadly, you are not the very best.

"Like no one ever was."

When we move from school to university, we suddenly realise that there are people smarter than us. Universities select the best of the best and suddenly you could be merely average in your year group. Practice is the same. They select the best of the best, who were likely the best of the best previously. You are now amongst the elite. It's naive to believe you are still the best in that scenario.

"You still do though."

I know I went in believing I was the best. I was very wrong. I thought my previous experience, my breadth of knowledge and my personality would set me apart from the rest. Sadly, everyone else also had those qualities and I was back in the pit, fighting for survival.

EXAM

The recruitment process is the first level of attrition. Those without a degree from university cannot apply to be part of any intake. I am aware this has changed slightly now due to an increased interest in vocational qualifications and a decreasing number of students applying.

Next there is a filter of online tests that check whether you have basic skills in communication, logic and literature. After that, the initial interview weeds out those who don't fully appreciate what they are signing up for and what is important for the role. Next, an assessment day and Partner interview remove those who don't fit the culture of the firm. Finally, you must achieve your predicted grades at university to be awarded your position even after this whole process.

After all of this. There is a sigh of relief. You've made it. You're in. You're safe.

Nope.

"The fuck?"

You are now studying for your qualification to become a Chartered Accountant.[10] This involves numerous exams alongside several hundred days of on-the-job experience.

"Doesn't sound too bad. We've done exams, we can do them again."

This time though, it's two strikes and you're out. This is how it was for me. Some practices are more lenient,

---

[10] www.icaew.com Accessed on 30/08/19

some are stricter. Regardless, failure is failure and if you fail to pass the exams in accordance with your contract you lose your job and may be required to repay the costs associated with your courses to date.

"Sounds a little harsh."

Also, your results are public, and you will be openly and directly ranked against your peer group and therefore forced to compete.

Have fun, good luck, let's see if you make it.

The pressure is on.

LOSS

This to me is the hardest part of becoming an accountant and working in practice. Others probably don't find it so hard, but I have this stupid character trait that I was told was a weakness, where I care about people. I care about other people a hell of a lot.

I failed three out of my first six exams. I told myself excuses at the time: they were multiple choice, there were no errors carried forward, each choice could reasonably be calculated with a simple error in a calculation or by simply misreading one word in a sentence.

"What about the fact you just didn't work hard enough?"

It was brutal.

I felt so much pressure to succeed, not just from the firm, not just from the Partners, nor just from my peer group or even just from myself. I also felt pressure from my friends and family. Whether only perceived or real, that pressure made me work harder than I had ever done before. That pressure made me want to succeed. I spent countless hours each night revising and preparing. I would work and study at weekends. I would go to the office at weekends to study just for a change of scenery as it was too distracting being at home.

People joke that studying for your qualification is akin to signing the death sentence of your social life for two years. I didn't believe them.

I was wrong.

> *"Nothing but passing those exams mattered. We'll make up the time with all the people we leave behind when we get these exams passed. They'll forgive us. We won't miss much. It'll be okay. Won't it?"*

Luckily, I passed the second sittings of those three exams and continued to pass the remaining nine exams on the first attempt to get my qualification.

Others weren't so lucky.

Others were fired.

Others lost their jobs within six weeks of starting.

Others lost their jobs after over a year with the firm.

It was heartbreaking.

The pain, suffering and sorrow everyone felt was unbelievable. There were tears almost every day of college, both from people being fired and from the pressure placed on each person to pass these exams. Some people broke and just dropped out; others valiantly stayed on to the bitter end until they were removed like weeds.

All for what?

A qualification?

A bit of paper to put on a wall?

At numerous times throughout my time at college, I said to myself, 'I don't even care if I fail now, I just want this done.' I wasn't alone in saying this either. We were all broken. Those scenes in movies of army cadets being broken down and then built back up in the model image of the army? It was that.

> *"It was worth it. It was definitely worth it. I'm a Chartered Accountant. I'm an Associate of the Institute of Chartered Accountants of England and Wales. I qualified at a Big Four accounting firm. It makes me stand out. Right?"*

I won't deny the value of that little bit of paper that I have framed on my wall hanging next to my bachelors and masters degrees. My career and successes are based on that qualification.

But was it worth it?

Yes.

No.

At the time, the qualification will feel like everything to you. It will drive you to do things you never believed you were capable of doing. I've said before that I wouldn't change my past as it's allowed me to become who I am today, but if I was asked if I wanted to do another qualification now in that style, the answer would be a resounding no because my mental health and wellbeing are far more important to me now.

> *"Not just yourself though. The people around you saw you go through this and felt your pain too."*

BOON

As you are going through this process, you will question your motivations and decisions. It is a natural response to the pressure you are under. Qualifications for any professional body are hard. Members need to be committed and this is an easy way to ensure all members are committed and of the same capability.

You will need to learn how to spin many plates. As time goes on more and more plates will need to be kept spinning at once. You will be balancing your exams, your studies, your work, your projects and your life!

Initially in your organisation, you are an unknown. One thing you should remember, and it isn't something particularly nice to hear, is that you are a resource and will be treated as such. At least to begin with anyway!

> *"It is called Human Resources for a reason."*

Sounds shit, doesn't it?

Professional services live and die by their people and you are one of them. You will be moved as needed to achieve what the organisation needs to achieve. As much as you will hear about flexibility and freedom, you will not be in control of your decisions. Or at least won't be in control of them for a while.

Again, this isn't necessarily bad.

Focus on changing what you can control rather than worrying about what you can't. You will spend much fewer spoons, waste much less time and likely be much happier consequently. It won't necessarily make things easier at the time, but it will allow you to focus your efforts on the fights worth fighting.

In my opinion, the only fights ever worth fighting are those over you!

Cultures and Cliques: Bullying, Belittling and Banter

JOIN

In a culture and environment built on survival of the fittest and structured a bit like a college, we should probably go back to the school yard to see if we can find where success comes from.

At school, children who are born in September and October, the beginning of the school year, typically outperform those born towards the back end of the school year, in June through August. This is simply because they are older and have had more time to develop and grow. Even though they're older by just a few months, it can often have a huge impact on activities such as reading and sports.

Rather than age, this is the equivalent of experience when looking at practice. So how do you get the upper hand on experience? Well, many accounting firms now offer summer internships ahead of your final year at university. The premise is twofold: do the interview process early and offer the best of those interns a job to start when they finish their degrees.

Recruitment requirements are now lower for the following year and you have brought on some extra resource on the cheap whilst your current employees go away on holiday over the summer. Practices that offer this get a great deal out of the arrangement and yet students fight over these places even more fiercely than the actual graduate opportunities that will be available to them later. It is quite ridiculous how much they are valued!

"You could probably even ask the students to pay the firm for the opportunity, creating a new revenue stream. Then it would be win-win-win for the firm."

Those successful enough to make it onto a summer internship become gods in their new peer group.

They know the job already. They know what they're doing and therefore can do it faster and without significant training. This leads to them being picked for more complex jobs and clients, which in turn accelerates their status. They are also known by the staff and those requesting resource for their jobs. Not only are they favoured for their ability, they are also favoured for their personality. Finally, they know the way things work in the office.

Office dynamics are hard to spot when you start in a new role. Regardless of what an organisational structure says, there are certain people that have a position in an organisation that far outweighs their pay grade.

Secretaries to Partners are the gatekeepers to success. Reception staff, janitors and security are the holders of convenience. Human Resources, Information Technology and the mail room or printing staff are the defenders of your time. These are the people you need on your side as much as possible.

Why?

These people are entirely office-based and keep everything running. These people speak to everyone else in an organisation. These people talk. Secretaries have access to Partner calendars and mailboxes. They might even have access to yours. They know everything that is going on. The holders of convenience are the people who can help make your life easier, assisting with booking car parking spaces, gaining access to the office on weekends, logistical issues etc. Finally, those that defend your time can make or break your success. They determine how smoothly your jobs go, how efficiently things happen and what the finished articles look like.

With these people on your side, you can do anything. Those who have stronger relationships with them will be better positioned for the future. These are the people who also deserve the utmost respect from everyone in any organisation as the firm would fail and crumble to dust without them.

Do you think a Partner would be able to submit their own expenses report or fix their own laptop? No. Just wouldn't happen. These people are the heroes of every organisation and it is in them that the real power lies.

GANG

At High School there are a lot of cliques and tropes. Unfortunately, these persist through university and into the professional workplace. Thinking back there was a broad trifecta.

The cool kids.

The geeks.

The outsiders.

These can all be categorised by how they seek acceptance.

The cool kids seek acceptance from others. They try to fit in with what is socially acceptable and what is popular. The geeks seek acceptance from their work and their results. The outsiders seek acceptance for being different.

No category is correct.

No category has an advantage.

Understanding them, however, is what is important as it will mean you can stand out within your category. As always it comes down to knowing yourself and knowing where you are and where you want to be within the grand design of the world.

This categorisation is also where a lot of the competition comes from. It's also, dare I say it, what can lead to bullying.

Bullying is a strong word. We associate it most with what happens in playgrounds. One kid physically bullies another kid, maybe knocking him to the ground or kicking him in the shin.

*"Or slicing open the back of your leg with a razor blade
wanting to see if fat drips out?"*

True story!

This is a very outdated form of bullying.

What happens nowadays is far worse and has a much more lasting impact than cuts, scrapes and scars.

*"Sticks and stones may break our bones, but names will
never hurt us."*

Remember this rhyme?

The issue is names and verbal insults do hurt us. They hurt us invisibly in a way that may not even hurt until days, weeks, months, even years down the line. I remember people at school who called me fat used to say to me, 'Oops too big, have to go sideways.' I still remember it. I think about it every time I have to turn sideways to reach something. It's funny what sticks with us. Bullying nowadays is even worse than name calling. It's passive aggressive actions like not tagging people in a picture on social media, not inviting them to a group chat, sending a snapchat of them behind their back. All these things are subtle and to a wise old soul like me would mean nothing.

*"You're still not being invited to places or involved in
chats."*

There is a serious problem with this form of bullying occurring in our schools right now.

I can't discuss it here as it probably needs an entire book in itself but know that it is happening.

This is the sort of bullying that takes place within practices. This is bullying designed to undermine you and your confidence without ever appearing to be negative. It's insidious. It's everywhere. It's happening right now.

BULL

Story time.

"Great. Sigh."

It was my birthday. I believe I was turning twenty-five at the time. I was working at a client's office that was about an hour away from where I lived. It was an awkward commute. I had been out the night before for dinner with my family to celebrate. It was the only night they could do. I enjoyed it.

During the day, I received a phone call. It was one of my friends. They had organised a surprise meal out for my birthday. It was a nice gesture and I was excited to see them.

I told the others in the room. Most ignored it and just carried on with the work. The woman in charge, however, said something along these lines: 'What? You're going out for a second birthday meal? Guess that's okay, the rest of us working late here will pick up your slack.'

"Fuck off."

This is what is wrong in practice.

This is passive aggressive bullying at its finest.

Let's break it down.

"Hammer time?"

Firstly, there is an assumption that you can only celebrate your birthday once and that celebrating it more than once is somehow unrealistic. Secondly, I was not asking for permission and was not seeking approval to go. Next there is a belief that I am slacking, when I was ahead with my work. Finally, there is this thick layer of guilt added about working late.

I now feel bad about something that was meant to be fun and enjoyable.

This happened time and time again. Different people, different words, same sentiment. You should feel guilty because you are having fun and others are still working. This is jealousy. This is envy. This is wrong. The fact that I remember it so well and can name the person involved – don't worry, I won't – should help demonstrate how much it affected me.

Rather than be jealous, envious or in the most extreme circumstances purely malicious, why not just congratulate the person who's getting to do something enjoyable and fun? Tell them to enjoy it and to get a break and to relax. They'll value that a lot more and will in turn reciprocate the feeling to others. Simple changes in what we speak and how we act can have a huge impact on the lives and wellbeing of those around us.

Next up is a rather simple tale.

Again, I was working as part of a team with a client. This one was a little further away so required the team to stay in a hotel nearby. We would go out for dinner as a team. It was good. Doing this enables you to build actual friendships and relationships with those people you work with in a non-work setting.

We were sat for dinner in a Thai restaurant. It was a really nice experience with sunken seating, enabling you to sit at the appropriate height as if you were cross legged. Midway through the meal, as is normal, someone asked whether we were enjoying the food.

> *"Always happens. Conversation grinds to a halt. Then all you talk about is food."*

I responded, saying it was good and I was enjoying it. Another voice said, 'I bet you like a lot of food, don't you?' I started replying that I do love food and that I really enjoy cooking and baking. I was interrupted before I could finish by someone saying, 'You can't ask him that.' Why not? Suddenly I felt I had missed the joke. 'Sorry, he didn't mean that.' What the hell was happening?

After dissecting the conversation, it was because I was fat.

> *"Fatty, fat, fat, fat."*

I couldn't be asked about whether I liked food or not as I might see it as an insult. I didn't care. I didn't care up until the point someone else tried to defend me as if being fat was taboo. I suddenly felt extremely self-conscious about what I was eating and how much I was eating. It felt awful. It was ridiculous, but again, it was unconscious bullying.

Here is another, less subtle, example of workplace bullying.

If it isn't obvious by now, I am definitely an outsider. I enjoy being quirky and having an offbeat personality. To that end, I enjoy collectable trading card games. To those unaware, think Pokémon cards.

> *"Yes. I had a foil Charizard. I had many. I sold them and my full collections recently and made a small fortune."*

I enjoyed these for the games and the strategy, not for the collection. At the time I would describe it as a game of chess where you got to customise the pieces you brought to the table.

It all started on Facebook with the upcoming release of a new expansion for the card game I was playing at the time. We were in the middle of spoiler season, where new cards are shown to build excitement and anticipation, and I saw a new card that was released for the first time. It was awful. People on social media were saying it was unplayable and questioning why they would print it.

> *"Hmmm. This reminds me of something from another game. Very similar design."*

I quickly searched through the list of available cards to see if the counterpart to the other combo piece existed in this game. If it did, I was onto something.

It did.

> *"We broke the format!"*

As with everything on the internet and social media, as soon as you know something you have to tell the world about it and make sure that you are the first person to do so. You earn invisible geek kudos points for it, I believe.

So, I did. I started a discussion thread and the community for the game at large started discussing what I had found out and how to maximise it. It felt good.

Later I checked my phone and saw three people from my firm had posted on the thread as well. Odd. They didn't strike me as people who played card games. I looked at the posts and it was sarcasm, insults and bullying. There was nothing positive. My heart sank. Not only had I been embarrassed, they were cool kids which meant the gossip would flow round the office like wildfire. I was ashamed and upset. Suddenly something I cared about, loved and was good at was a source of pain, embarrassment and shame. It didn't take long for me to stop playing entirely in an attempt to fit in. Self-sacrifice for the professional service.

Now the three men in question are all incredibly successful. All have made it to Partner or Partner-level positions across the globe in various organisations. All are likely now promoting positive mental health amongst their staff and organisations. All have likely forgotten about the day they bullied that other guy for being a geek.

The only person who hasn't forgotten that day is this geek.

Me.

I have no doubt that this was just done for 'banter' purposes.

> *"Seriously. Insulting people isn't banter. It's just insulting people. Banter requires back and forth and knowing that it is okay to begin with. Stop it."*

I have no doubt that it wasn't meant to hurt me in the way it did. I have no doubt that if I asked for an apology, they would give it.

The point is that this shouldn't happen in the first place. This action made me resent working with these people. This action along with countless similar actions across the years made me feel unwelcome and unable to continue at my firm. Even though those people left and moved on, the fact they were part of the in crowd made me feel like I wasn't welcome at all.

I could continue telling you tens if not hundreds of stories of people insulting me in different ways over the years of my career. It won't add to the point that is already clear though: your words have consequences and can hurt people.

Many will say that I need to get a thicker skin. Just brush it off. Ignore it. Water off a dog's back and all.

"That's an in-joke too far, my friend."

Thing is, I took everything people said and then some. It seemed as if I had a pretty thick skin. Brazen arrogance and faux self-confidence allowed me to take it and brush it off. Nowadays, under the shadow of suicide, I genuinely don't care what other people think anymore.

"Sticks and stones may break my bones, but words will leave a lasting impact on my mental health that will haunt me for the rest of my life."

Was this bullying part of what drove me to contemplate suicide?

Probably not.

Was this bullying part of what caused me to have low confidence, low self-esteem and a low feeling of self-worth, ultimately making me resent myself?

Definitely.

Your Comfy Pants

COOL

Despite knowing all this is going to happen one way or another it won't make it any easier at the time. Sadly, this is always the case with knowing about your mental health and understanding your emotions. Even though you know you shouldn't feel like that and that it's irrational or incorrect, it doesn't make it easier to stop! You may well be able to brush off the negativity and wear a genuine smile, laughing at the 'banter'.

I wasn't.

It ate away at my personality over the years. It made me feel that I wasn't meant to be there and that I was never going to fit in no matter how much I tried.

Slowly but surely my personality corroded.

I'm here to tell you that you don't have to feel this way. You can avoid the pain I felt, and if I'm honest still feel, by simply remembering something that I never thought.

You are enough.

I wish I'd known these three words when I was working in the Big Four.

I wish I'd believed these words.

Even though I was happy being an outsider, I always wanted to get noticed. I wanted to stand out. I wanted attention. We all want to receive praise. It's natural. It's not bad. Hearing good things about us makes us happy. The problem is when these wants and desires come at the expense of your personality.

"We gave up a lot of that over the years."

Whoever you are. Whatever you are doing. Have confidence in yourself.

"How can you say that when you have no confidence in yourself?"

You are unique and no one can ever claim otherwise.

No matter what anyone else says about you always remember that you are enough.

AREA

Other people are always welcome to have their opinions. They are welcome to share them. This is the freedom of speech much of our society is based upon.

"Haters gonna hate, right?"

If you enjoy something, thrive in it. If you want to do something, find a way to do it. We all have different strengths and weaknesses and the key to standing out in a professional organisation is to double down on your strengths whilst slowly challenging your weaknesses.

Here is where we will begin to talk about fulfilment.

I'll say this now just in case: fulfilment is not a crime! You can feel happy, content and fulfilled in life! You can settle for second best. You can be the first loser.

> *"You're the biggest loser I know!"*

It's okay!

To begin to find your fulfilment you need to not only ask yourself what you are good at; you also need to ask yourself whether you enjoy it. I mean really enjoy it. Not just sit there and let it pass by saying 'it's okay' daily. Do you really enjoy it?

At this stage in my career, when I was coming towards the end of my qualification and finishing my exams, all I cared about was what I was good at.

I tell a lie.

I cared about what I was good at and what I didn't enjoy. I wasn't thinking at all about what I did enjoy, only what I didn't. I didn't enjoy assurance, that's for a sure.

> *"Are you really going to have poor grammar in a book to make a bad pun? Fuck's sake, your standards have slipped."*

This is the worst motivation when looking at making changes in your career. It leads to poor decisions and often several quick changes without any real growth and development. Career opportunities will be covered in more detail later, but just know that my motivations when trying to find my niche were not entirely pure and weren't necessarily correct in hindsight. I wouldn't change them, but I would maybe have thought more about the options in front of me.

> *"Hindsight is often twenty-twenty, but more often than not rose-tinted."*

When looking to prioritise your strengths, what you are seeking to find is your niche. What are you good at? What can you do that others can't, or at least can do better than others? Finding your niche allows you to become a specialist. Being a specialist means that you are needed and wanted for that specialist skill set. It's a great place to be.

I still call myself a corporate finance[11] specialist to this day, even though I'm shit at it and knowing that there is nothing that special about it. There are some big and fancy words, confusing acronyms, complex Excel models simplified to the point of data entry and then the traditional bullshit sales chat.

> *"It's a dark art! You're a wizard, Andy."*

Once you're part of the secret society and know the handshake, that's it, you're set.

Finding your specialism can be tricky though. You might end up as a specialist in an area you don't really like. I developed a reputation for my work and knowledge around net-debt and the pet food sector.

---

[11] www.icaew.com/technical/corporate-finance Accessed on 30/08/19

"Don't ask. I didn't even have pets at the time!"

People would ask me questions about areas I was supposedly an expert in because I had applied some knowledge on one or two projects.

If you can find your niche and your specialism then you can thrive.

EDIT

I am adding this now, during edits, because I feel it needs to be said.

"Breaking the Fourth Wall much?"

I no longer find happiness in being a specialist. I thought I did, but I am a generalist through and through. I like consolidating vast amounts of disjointed information and pulling it all together. I like sitting back and seeing the big picture move and flow. I enjoy finding patterns in actions and reactions. I love solving puzzles!

"You like writing in the first person in short sentences to add emphasis!"

At this point in my career I wanted to be a specialist as I wanted to stand out. Now I'm happy blending in.

Just as my opinions and feelings changed, so might yours.

So, keep listening to yourself and never be afraid to make a change that feels right to you!

CHAT

Once you understand what you want to do and where you want to focus, it is then all about making it happen.

"But I don't want to!"

Yep.

You are going to need to motivate yourself for this. No one will make it happen for you. This is all about you driving the change you want to see through to completion.

It's not easy.

But you can do it! You can make it happen!

Communication and being open are the most important things to make any of this change happen. You should speak to your manager and potentially even their manager to ensure you are working towards where you want to be.

Working towards something you don't want and don't enjoy is miserable and can cause you to get stuck in a painful cycle.

No one else is going to fight for your future. People may talk about supporting you on your journey, but no one is really going to put your happiness and success ahead of their own. It would be nice to believe they will, but I promise you: push comes to shove, you are less important than them.

The only exception to this is in love.

"What?"

But that's for another book.

"We're writing more?"

EXIT

FOUR

PROMOTION, PREMONITION AND MAKING A PLAN

White Collars Can't Jump

ANTE

Promotion and climbing up the corporate ladder is often in the forefront of our minds whilst working in practice.

When can I take on the next challenge?

When will I be recognised for what I'm doing?

When can I get a pay rise and afford whatever new and shiny thing it is I want?

It's partly due to our desire as humans to be rewarded and recognised for our work, but it's also driven into us as part of the collegiate system.

Practice tells us that the goal is to make it to Partner.

If you don't make it to Partner, what are you even doing in the firm?

You've failed!

This chapter provides an in-depth look at the structure of partnerships and how they go from the ridiculous to the sublime as seemingly the only organisations that ask manufacturing specialists to move into sales for promotion.

In practice you often hear whispers around the office about 'Who's going for Partner?' or 'Did you hear that they didn't make it because…?' You might hear whispers of 'career Directors' or 'career Managers' as if that is their place in life.

It can be horrible.

One of the Partners I worked with repeatedly used the expression 'Onwards and upwards'.

"That and how our team was 'small but perfectly formed'."

There was only one trajectory.

"If you remember, they actually used the catchphrase 'Velocity: More than Distance over Time'. It is by definition! Velocity is a vector. It requires a trajectory!"

If you weren't on this path, then it was probably time you walked another. Looking back, this messaging is far more damaging than it is motivating. I appreciated it at the time, thrived off it in fact. Now I understand it more. That drive stopped me from seeing what mattered to me and it blinded me to the warning signs in my head!

The problem with a trajectory is that there is a chance of failure. What if you are not moving onwards or upwards? What if you're going downwards? What if you aren't in control at all?

It is the same as when people say they want to 'fight' mental health. Fighting by its nature implies there is a winner or a loser,

"Or that you are caught in an eternal battle with no winner or loser. That's arguably a better descriptor of our loving relationship."

and as such if you don't win and overcome your struggles, then by definition you are the loser, compounding the negativity.

It's why I talk about acceptance a lot.

It's why acceptance in your job and in yourself is important.

It's why understanding the collegiate system, the structure and the roles of each grade and the rewards system in place is important.

It's why this chapter exists!

Over the years, many people have said to me that I would be a great Partner in a professional practice.

"Your mum doesn't count!"

My problem isn't that I wouldn't be a great Partner, it is that I am a terrible Associate through Senior Manager. I am not a great 'do-er', no matter how much I say I am. I get bored of repetition. I get tired from lack of engagement. I get lost in detail and just stop caring. Sorry, not sorry, to all those people I lied to over the years saying that I love being in the detail. I don't!

It's also why I'm no good at anything involving the 'monthly cycle' of finance. It's repetitive and boring. If it's something we're doing repeatedly, why can't we just automate it?

So, here's the rub.

"A spicy rub?"

You can't jump from one grade to another. You can't bypass grades that you aren't good at. You just can't.

"Skip to the end."

To compound this, each grade fundamentally requires different things. Associates and Senior Associates do.

There isn't much more to it than this. They are the assembly workers in a factory making whatever it is that is being made. Partners on the other hand are the Sales and Marketing team. They don't do, they sell.

Production and Sales are two very different skill sets. Both are incredibly important, and neither could function without the other. So why in a regular manufacturing business do we not see a similar drive from Production towards Sales?

Structure.

Specialism.

And Reward.

In a practice there are typically six grades: Associate, Senior Associate, Manager, Senior Manager or Associate Director, Director and Partner. There are numerous grades within Partner, but we're not going to consider those for now. Six grades in the grand scheme of things is a relatively flat structure. Also, each of these grades is rewarded very differently and a move from one grade to another can have a significant impact on your monthly disposable income.

In a manufacturing company, there can be many more grades that are far more varied. New grades and roles can even be created at the whims of management. These grades and the rewards attached to them can be very similar and adjusted ad hoc to make sure people are motivated and rewarded correctly. Moving from Production to Sales might not even change your disposable income. There are numerous tiers within Production that can generate small, incremental changes to your disposable income;

and likely moving from Production to Sales will result in you starting from the beginning and then beginning the climb up the ladder all over again.

This is one of the most important things I didn't understand about practice whilst I was working there. I focused purely on the promotions and trying to 'skip to the end'. It just doesn't work that way.

"Curse those well-oiled red tape machines!"

What I should have focused on was challenging myself to be the best at each grade I was at the time before thinking about moving to the next one.

"Would you have actually done that though?"

Nope!

Practice life is a structured life. Outside of practice things can get a little wild. Regardless of where you work, everything comes down to your ability to influence. I believe that those who work hard and deliver results deserve the appropriate reward; however, what it boils down to is those who show they work hard and show they deliver results get the rewards.

Showing and doing are two very different things; the former of which doesn't necessarily even need to be based on the latter.

Influence matters!

With all promotions in practice, you pretty much need to be already doing the job you want before you'll get promoted into it and rewarded for it.

> *"The whole point of growing as an individual is being
> out of your comfort zone, yet here you're asked to be
> comfortable already."*

We'll now go on to look at the individual grades, where their focus lies and what you need to think about if you want to consider going for a promotion or not.

MAKE

Let's begin at the beginning.

Associates and Senior Associates do. They are the brute force that makes everything tick in practice. Without them, there would be no 'resource' and no 'flex' on any projects; the gears would stop turning and the clock would just simply stop.

They are new to the firm and often new to working life, with many coming straight from university. They are likely on their training contracts and some may still be studying for the exams to achieve their qualification.

Most importantly, they are still learning.

And whilst learning, even the mundane can be made exciting!

> *"Possibly the most soulless thing you've written in this
> book."*

Qualifications take a set number of days to complete and therefore Associates and Senior Associates must do all the work they can to reach their time quota. It doesn't matter whether it's doing something interesting such as financial modelling and forecasting, or whether it is the worst thing in existence imaginable, like counting gas in Hull on New Year's Eve at midnight that literally only requires the reading of nine numbers from a control panel, which can probably be done with a webcam or computer vision software.

"Weirdly specific, dude. You okay?"

These roles are about production and delivery of work. You need to do what is required of you in a timely fashion and to a high standard. It is important you learn the art of self-review and time management.

Self-review is easier than it sounds.

I suck at it.

I still feel sorry for the copy editor who worked on this book!

"Duck 'em. Duck it. Duck this. Ducking auto-correct!"

Whilst doing, you also need to take time to step back and make sure everything is documented correctly and in line with any required compliance methodology and guidelines. In practice there is often a very strict internal audit or risk and compliance function that ensures all work is carried out to the required standards in the industry.[12] Make sure you know what this is and that you abide by it.

"Good thing that such good practice guidance exists, otherwise we might end up with huge listed clients of

---

[12] www.frc.org.uk Accessed on 31/08/19

Big Four audit practices going into administration every year!"

Time management is important to keep yourself on track, but also important in protecting your time. If you do not learn to manage the time of your bosses, or reviewers, then you are subject to the unknown and can leave yourself 'waiting for the reply' in dread.

This is bad for your mental health. It can lead to anxiety and stress.

The simplest way to address this is to allocate yourself the time you need to do a task whilst also blocking out time for your manager to review the work. By allocating yourself the appropriate time to complete your work and your manager the appropriate time to review it, you have reduced the net workload, net uncertainty and net stress for you both.

Doing all of this will build your confidence. Others will develop trust in you as you're holding yourself accountable and making their life easier as you are demonstrating you don't need to be managed.

Taking responsibility for your actions is incredibly important and this is where you need to learn and demonstrate that.

FULL

Many people view the Manager grade as the toughest role in all of practice and I believe this is largely true. I believe this is mostly due to it meaning different things to different people within different departments.

Let's start with this.

Manager implies you manage.

"Manage to survive? Manage to escape?"

What most people perceive 'manage' to mean is that they manage people. What it means is you manage time. There is a dramatic difference in what these mean and how they operate so it's no wonder people believe this is one of the hardest roles.

As an Associate or Senior Associate, you have someone managing your time. They tell you what work you're doing, for how long and when it needs to be complete. You then just get on and do it.

You do!

As a Manager, you are responsible for all the above, but now you must allocate your time across several of these projects at the same time.

Oh.

You also need to manage people.

You must manage the time and delivery of the work from Associates and Senior Associates. It's why it is so important to learn good time management early on. You will be managing time for the rest of your career.

By managing others and their time, you have also taken on responsibility for the delivery of their results. If they fuck up, that's on you. If they fuck around, that's on you. If they fuck off, guess who's picking up the work!

The worst part is that as well as all the time management, you also need to do your own work.

You are now experiencing what it is like to be an entrepreneur.

You are manufacturing your product and selling it. This is where a lot of people struggle as they cannot balance this dichotomy as well as they believe they should.

> *"I really want you to use the word anathema here, but can't think of a way to fit it in. Curse these italics and not letting me have actual narrative control!"*

If you are in this position and are struggling, don't worry, it's natural. You have been trained for three to five years to do and are now being asked to not only do yourself, but to enable others to do. Time is finite. Energy is finite. You're doing more and more. This is the point at which most people choose to move on.

Why?

It's designed that way.

The net difference in reward between Senior Associate and Manager is not that significant. However, the net difference in workload is incredibly significant. The move from Manager to Senior Manager in reward is significant, so better to have those who are unable to survive in the 'battle royale' move on as soon as possible.

It's sneaky!

It's duplicitous!

It's accounting and legal practices through and through!

BOND

You've made it through to Senior Manager.

"Associate Director."

I've heard it both ways.

You've proven you're technically excellent. You can do. You can manage your time and the time of others.

What now?

Time to start again.

"Huh?!"

You've now moved to the Sales and Marketing department as an intern but still must maintain all your responsibilities from Production.

"Wait, what?"

Doesn't sound fair, does it?

This is where your ability to sell and influence will be really tested. This is often the maximum grade that can be reached by someone who is purely technically orientated without the capability, or personality, for selling.

This is also where your commitment to your firm will be tested the most and will be the death knell for many who are on the edge about whether they are committed to the firm and its ideals or not.

Your ability to progress from here will be determined by your influence with those outside of your firm. You will need to focus on selling your firm, developing your network, bringing in reliable leads and finally converting and completing your projects. To make the move further up you need to still be delivering but need to be doing it alongside winning new work.

It can take a good few years to fully adapt to becoming a salesperson. Don't worry if you are not a natural at it. Sales is a skill you can learn. Equally though, if you don't want to learn how to sell, don't be afraid to admit it!

TEST

Director is where things really get interesting.

You've proven your worth to the firm, can deliver jobs, manage people well, market the firm as a whole and also may be generating your own sales and profit margin, just with it being allocated to someone else.

Partnership is very much what it says on the tin.

It's a partnership.

You and your Partners are working together, sharing the good times with the bad. By becoming a member of the partnership, you are allowing your success to be tied to those others in your firm. This is an important decision to make and one that is not to be taken lightly.

I have known Directors who have chosen to stay Directors because they wanted to keep the status quo. I have known Directors who have tried to make Partner multiple times and been rejected every time. I've known Directors who have been forced out and told they will never make Partner. Similarly, I've known Directors who have been told this and then pushed on to make Partner despite the criticism.

Here it's all about determination and how much you want it!

Can you taste it yet?

As a Director you are essentially a Partner-in-waiting. You need to prove time and again that you can bring in work, manage your profitability and manage your people. Once you have done this it is your choice as to whether to take the next step or not.

Would I do it if I had stuck it out?

Probably not.

Whilst the allure of the reward would be appealing and the work would be far more in line with what I enjoy, I think I would ultimately still be unhappy with the life. I think it's more about what organisation I'd be a Partner in than whether I'd become a Partner or not.

Only you will know what to do when the opportunity arises.

Long-Term Incentives

SELL

All jobs in all industries dovetail towards the same single role regardless of risk, reward or rank. This might sound ridiculous, but you only need to look at a few companies before you realise it is true.

Let's start small: in an entrepreneurial owner-managed business, everything comes back to that single owner and their ability to influence people to buy their product.

Once money is coming in, it translates to their ability to lead others to continue to develop and deliver those products, whilst they continue selling their products and growing the business further!

Moving to a slightly larger company, maybe with some private equity or bank funding behind it, the person at the top is now influencing not only sales, but also the investors. They still lead, they still manage, but fundamentally their responsibilities are to ensure the business has enough funding to continue growth. This funding can be from sales or from financing, but it is the same thing being sold, the business and its products.

Even as we approach large listed entities with lots of regulation and structure around them, the person at the top focuses on the relationships with investors and funding providers as well as ensuring that sales continue to be delivered.

There is no escaping it.

You can run from it.

You can hide from it.

But it is inevitable.

"Alright, Thanos."

At the end of the day, if your dreams and ambitions are to be at the top of an organisation, then you need to learn to sell.

LEAD

I was told whilst I was at school that it wasn't the A-grade students that would be the leaders of tomorrow; the C-grade students would end up at the top with the A-grade students working for them.

"Why are we working so hard then?"

I laughed, thinking it was absolute nonsense.

What did my teachers know about business?

I was going to get good grades and be a leader!

I'd prove them wrong.

"How the mighty have fallen!"

Now clearly this isn't always true. There are plenty of smart and technically minded people who have made it to the top.

So why is it even said?

Often those people who have lower grades need to rely more on their personality. They don't necessarily have the natural intellect or learned ability to influence what they want, so they rely on their charm and charisma.

This becomes their tradecraft.

The C-grade students don't need to retrain or learn new skills when they want to move up in an organisation; they have practised the art of influencing for many years.

The A-grade students aren't as natural at bullshitting so take their time studying, learning and practising it.

The natural intuition built by the C-grade students wins out and they float towards the top, like bubbles in a beer.

None of this is to say that it is impossible for A-grade students to become leaders or influencers; just that the sooner one can start working on salesmanship and the ability to influence and sell, then the easier it will be when it becomes the time to start selling.

Salesmanship is a skill like any other and if you want to maintain a level of excellence you have to practise constantly.

"You're lying if you think this isn't the most niche reference in this book."

I get called a puppeteer by some people. It's not a name I like, but it's a name I have earned through my style of influencing. I often do not sit at the top making decisions – that's a lot of responsibility and I'm lazy. I often float around the top pulling the strings of others, subtly moving the dominoes through the house of cards to hit the bullseye.

"Check mate!"

Nowadays people just want to become one of those influencers who just pose with bottles

"…and likely lines…"

of coke on a beach somewhere claiming they could never have a proper job because it would be too hard on them.

TWIN

Reward at the top of an organisation is a strange one.

If you've ever studied Maslow's Hierarchy of Needs,[13] you've now got everything apart from the very top of the pyramid complete. You are looking for self-actualisation. So, what the heck is this?

"It's surprisingly important."

This is about finding your happiness. This is about experiences and fulfilment.

"Don't spoil it too early."

When I was training there was a programme that Partners could attend that was called 'Leaving a Legacy'. It was all about how they wanted to be remembered, how they could leave their team in the best place possible for when they stepped down or moved on and what to think about when it comes to succession planning.

"Succession planning? But you'll be a Partner till you retire, right?"

Wrong.

It is becoming increasingly rare for Partners to reach retirement age within a practice. Partnerships are structured on survival of the fittest, with an ever-decreasing number of opportunities for progression as you move up. To facilitate having more people join the partnership, some people need to move on. It wouldn't

---

[13] 'A theory of human motivation'. *Psychological Review*, 50(4), 370-396

be commercially sound to have a cohort of thirsty Directors knocking on the partnership's door and not being accepted; another firm might poach them and then there would be lost earnings and growth potential.

Partnerships, like most businesses, incentivise their most senior employees and leadership teams with long-term value. You're remunerated well so more disposable income won't really change your lifestyle, so the best way to incentivise numerically is through long-term pay-outs, equity, pension or some other structuring that will see you generate more value even after your time at the firm is concluded.

> *"Can this not lead to an ever-increasing amount owed to ex-partnership members that needs to be paid out in cash by future member earnings, resulting in a time bomb waiting to happen?"*

Welcome to the pension time bomb, my friend.

Long-term pay-outs via options, shares, dividends or whatever all rely on one thing. The company must continue to exist to fulfil the obligation.

So, you are left with this conundrum:

If you want to ensure the value you are due, that you have worked hard to earn, that you have spent a lifetime building towards, is maximised, what legacy do you want to leave behind? What is your succession plan?

> *"I don't want to let anyone else control this. I want to control it!"*

Who better to leave your legacy to than yourself?

Who better to maintain the status quo and deliver your value to you than yourself?

This is why it is ever so hard to break the cultural norm within practice. You want to know you are leaving your legacy in safe hands. Not necessarily so they can't do with it what they want, but so that it can be maintained for you until you finally receive your value out.

Then who cares?

It's someone else's problem then.

"It's the circle of life."

So, who better to replace you than yourself?

Train people in your image. Help them grow with your values.

Leave them responsible for keeping your money flowing whilst you swan around various non-executive director roles and advisory board roles for the next generation of businesses.

You've done your time!

Promotion Time!

LOVE

We've covered a lot about what practice is like and what to consider at each grade, and even what to think about before it comes to promotion time. Before we make any decisions about whether to stand still, go for promotion or look for another job, let's look at our job and employer closely.

Imagine that your job is your romantic partner.

"Eewww."

In a relationship there is a lot of compromise, but the fundamental basis of any romantic relationship is that the two individuals become stronger together. They each provide the other with something they want and in doing so mutual happiness improves.

"It's about sex, right?"

Romance and love are tricky things as they mean different things to different people. It is said that there are five languages of love.[14] This is not porn; that comes in Chapter Eight. These languages are about how love is given and received.

"Sounds a lot like porn."

The Love Languages in short are: Words of Affirmation, Acts of Service, Giving of Gifts, Quality Time and Physical Touch. Some of these are more and less appropriate in a workplace environment, but the sentiment stands.

"Physical Touch in the office should probably be avoided."

In romance, in all relationships, there is give and take. Sometimes you give a present, and it doesn't quite hit the mark. Sometimes you do something, and create a memory that lasts a lifetime.

There can often be a mismatch in how someone likes giving love and how their partner likes receiving love.

---

[14] *The Five Love Languages: How to Express Heartfelt Commitment to Your Mate*. Chicago: Northfield Publishing

"Still sounds like porn."

I myself value Quality Time and Words of Affirmation more than anything else. I don't want for things and I don't want stuff done for me. Physical Touch is important to me, but what means the most is when someone chooses to spend their time with me and chooses to say nice things about me.

The complexity comes because I like the Giving of Gifts to people and performing Acts of Service. I will always say Words of Affirmation and spend Quality Time together, but to me, showing the subservience and the vulnerability that comes with it is what I feel demonstrates real love.

Physical Touch plays a part, but ultimately, the physical becomes frail and the emotional and intellectual remain.

This is what I care about.

Take this into a work environment; if your work rewards you with financial incentives like salary increases, options, equity, pension, bonuses and more, yet you don't want for extra money but want more time with your family, it doesn't matter how much financial reward you receive, you won't find happiness in it.

Similarly, on a fundamental level, if your workplace doesn't support positive mental health and the wellbeing of staff and this is important to you, what do you do?

If this was in a romantic relationship what would you do?

Let's replace the lack of support for positive mental health and discuss something that can often come up between two individuals in a relationship: religion!

"Careful now!"

Religion and going to service weekly can be incredibly important to some. If your partner denied you this opportunity, or didn't support you in going to service in any way, what would you do?

You'd hopefully start by talking to your partner, ask if they're religious? Maybe they'd consider going with you? Would they mind you going alone? It's an open conversation.

Imagine they say no to all the above, and that they don't want you to go to service either.

"What a dick!"

You're then in a tricky situation.

Do you put your partner and relationship ahead of your beliefs and religion? Which means more to you? You're forced to decide whether you should compromise your beliefs or your relationship.

Eventually you need to decide if you can live without either.

No one should ever be forced into this situation, but it happens time and again.

Your relationship with your employer should be no different at all. If you are not getting what you want from your career or role you should start with an open conversation:

Why am I not getting promoted? Where do you see me going in the firm? What do I need to do to achieve what I want? Where is my advancement capped?

How many of you speak this candidly with your managers?

"Another rhetorical question?"

Maybe you should start?

A level of honesty like this allows you better information to make decisions.

Once you start having open conversations, then you need to consider their responses and opinions with your personal beliefs. If you feel you are not necessarily being treated fairly, or are not receiving the recognition, or love, in a way you are happy with, then you are in the same position as in the romantic relationship.

You need to choose if you are willing to compromise what you believe in to stay in the same job or seek another job that will provide what you need.

"Sex? Right?"

This is the same as in a relationship. You are choosing your beliefs over the relationship that doesn't allow those beliefs. You have put what you want first and that will make you happier in the long run.

It may be hard to make this analogy make sense in your situation.

It was certainly hard enough to write it!

"Why did we bother? Good story?"

They do say that all good relationships are founded on good communication.

"Who are they?"

PLAN

You've made the decision that your current employer isn't right for you. You know they're not fulfilling your needs, wants or desires so you choose to move on.

Great!

You've made this decision and you should be happy knowing it is what you want.

Don't go into it blindly though.

Working with recruitment companies is tricky. As with all companies, they are driven by sales, and they are selling you! What this means is they will operate the same way that any salesperson would: fit the product to the customer and not necessarily worry about the wellbeing of the product.

You have been reduced to a commodity.

Pretty heartless.

Some recruitment companies will talk about how they focus on the individual seeking a job, or sometimes might even have something around positive mental health. This is all well and good. Just remember who is paying them!

Hint.

It's not you!

Most recruitment companies will receive their payment as a percentage of your placed salary. At least they'll be fighting for your commodity value. They just won't necessarily be fighting for your wellbeing. Once you've gone through interviews and the process, it's easy to get swallowed up and accept whatever is offered without taking the time to consider it.

This is what recruiters want to happen.

It is incredibly important to step back and review where you are. You're moving out of choice. Will this new position fulfil you and your wants? Is it only temporary? If it isn't right, don't be afraid to say no. The recruiter will be pushing you towards accepting, but if something isn't right, don't get swallowed up.

Stand up for yourself.

SOON

One of the niche things about the accounting and legal markets is that there are almost fixed cycles based around year groups and promotion times. This means there are points in the calendar year when there will be a sudden influx of professionals looking for new jobs. For me this was always around June. As soon as people were aware if they were getting promoted, they would start looking. Similarly, upon qualifying following your exams and time served,

"...sounds like a prison..."

people would also leave. The market would flood with 'newly qualifieds'. Not only were you competing with your peer group for the internal promotion, you might actually be competing with them for an external role too!

Why is knowing this important?

Supply and demand.

When there is a larger quantity of a commodity the price is driven down. Which means placements will generate less value for you as the individual, but also your recruitment firm. Less care will go into the process. Your recruiter will likely be putting three to six candidates forward alongside you and doesn't really care which of you succeeds. They get paid regardless. You are in a much weaker position regardless of your personal strengths.

When there are fewer professionals in a market, you have more room to negotiate what you want and what you need. You are a rarer commodity and your recruiter needs to keep you on side as sales for such commodities will be fewer and farther between. It's the same with highly niche specialisms such as pensions. Fewer people have this experience, so you are inherently more valuable.

I can't tell you when the cycles are for your organisation, but you'll be able to find out easily. Plan for them. If you know it's going to be competitive between June and September, then either delay your move until after then or start the process earlier. Once you're clear on what you want, you are best to put the necessary actions into process.

Now for my usual controversial statement:

"Oh god."

In a world of perfect information, recruitment businesses shouldn't exist. They thrive on imperfect information and lack of available time. They survive on success and failure in a similar way to accountants and lawyers.

If you know you want to work for a particular company, try approaching them directly yourself rather than through a recruiter.

You'll have shown confidence in yourself and determination to achieve what you want. You've stated your intention openly and you're making the decision based on ethics and values rather than availability. You also don't have that recruitment fee attached.

Bargain!

Not only are you willing to fight for yourself, you come at a sizeable discount! And that discount can become part of your reward or used as an incentive. You have all the room in the world to negotiate!

It's up to you to fight for your own worth!

Put yourself first in these decisions and do what you want to do!

FIVE

THINKING BIG PICTURE IN A DETAIL-ORIENTATED WORLD

The World Is Not Your Oyster

NEWS

News Flash.

This just in.

The world is not your oyster.

> *"The fuck does that even mean? Who wants oysters?*
> *They're gross!"*

We are raised to believe that we can be anything. Our parents and schools teach us that we can grow up to be whatever we want.

Sadly, you can't.

Of all the children who say they want to be a doctor, or an astronaut, do you think they all make it? Of course not. Very few make it to live their childhood dreams.

> *"Do many people dream of being an accountant?"*

So why do we continue to say it? Wouldn't it be better to just embrace the mediocrity of life early on to avoid disappointment? Sorry, little Jimmy, you stand no hope of being a professional footballer. How about you look at being middle management in an insurance company?

This is a level of self-acceptance that unnerves some people. People want to achieve more! We are constantly looking for the next 'get rich quick scheme' as we seek to escape the inevitable onset of mediocrity.

This is partly why there are so many start-up companies nowadays; what better way to get rich quick and give the middle finger to a generation that lied to you since you were born, than by disrupting the economy they built with technology they don't fully understand?

This chapter focuses on reflection, regret and remorse. It's about looking back on your career objectively and trying to make sense of where you have come from and where you want to go next!

"A suicide booth?"

AWAY

Life is busy.

Life is always busy no matter what you're doing or where you are. That inner voice will be constantly chatting away, over and over, no matter what is going on.

> *"Hey, have you thought about what you're doing for dinner? You should probably eat healthy, but there's so little reason not to order takeaway. Yeah, order a takeaway. What about having a bath? You haven't had one of those in a while. Maybe we should cook dinner? Did you remember to put the bins out? Why aren't those shoes in a straight line? Fuck cooking dinner, let's just pick up chips on the way home."*

Whilst you're in the thick of it, it's hard to reflect properly. You will constantly be distracted by life. Taking that break that we always say we need is all well and good, but it isn't very effective if you don't relax and don't get the time to yourself that you want.

Time is the biggest hurdle here.

How long does it take you to properly relax and forget about life? How long does it take you to unwind?

For me it can take a while.

"I can't remember the last time we relaxed."

A long weekend? That's one day of travelling, a day of 'making the most' of being away, followed by another day of travelling and dreading the inevitable return to work tomorrow. There is no relaxation at all. You're just changing scenery and not needing to make meals or tidy up. You may go swimming or do something you wouldn't normally do, but the travel and anticipation of that dreaded Monday will consume any potential relaxation in no time.

A week to ten days? A day of travelling, a day of finding out what's in your vicinity and making a plan, a day of 'doing something because you're on holiday and you didn't stay at home for a reason', some relaxation time, a day of 'oh my god! I'm going home and back to my real life tomorrow', finally the day of travelling and preparation for that dreaded Monday. This sort of break typically yields between one and three days of relaxation.

"I hate holidays where you either do nothing or do something too often."

This continues.

From my experience you need about three whole weeks to be able to detach enough to properly relax. Two weeks comes close, but it's just that little bit short to fully let go.

The last time I had three weeks off.

Probably when I was at university.

"Probably why we're constantly exhausted!"

By stepping away from the complexities of life, you'll be better able to consider what matters.

Find your time to forget!

Then forget.

And enjoy your time.

LIKE

In professional practice, we're often taught about Maslow's Hierarchy of Needs.[15] It's a common way to explain what sort of reward will motivate someone.

"You briefly mentioned this before! Glad you're actually explaining it now!!"

The fundamental needs of humans are broken down into five categories: physiological, safety, emotional, esteem and self-actualisation.

We're taught that once one is achieved, a person can no longer be motivated in this way. If someone has all their physiological and safety needs met – i.e. they have a roof over their head and can provide for themselves – they will only really be motivated by emotional needs and above such as the sense of belonging.

Many people consider this in their career. A job needs to provide you with enough to survive and live comfortably.

---

[15] 'A theory of human motivation'. *Psychological Review*

Once you've got that, any other job must provide the sense of belonging to a team or the feeling of acknowledgement. Finally, once you have all this, your work should afford you the ability for self-development.

What if we flip it round?

Is it possible?

It's pyramid shaped for a reason!

With so much complexity and so much stress in life, why don't we start by searching for what we enjoy and what allows us to be our best selves? If we can find that and then look for a way to make it provide the other needs, then we end up much happier to begin with.

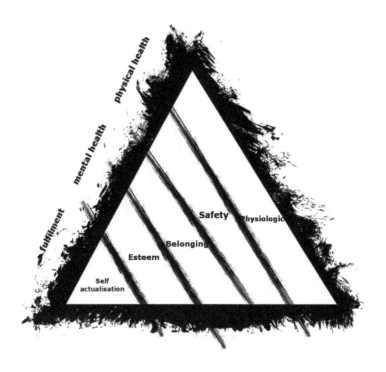

"Are you really so lazy you are going to leave those words partially obscured?"

What if instead of trying to climb a pyramid that gets harder and harder as you go up, instead we just start at self-actualisation and wander along the new base until we find our other needs?

Rather than starting at the basics of food, water and clothing, instead we find happiness and fulfilment.

Then our mental health is already taken care of. We are already becoming our best self by focusing on things like morality, creativity and acceptance. We will start by building self-esteem and confidence in ourselves. People with the same morality and acceptance will naturally accept us to provide our sense of belonging and in that belonging there will be safety and everything else we need.

It's certainly not easy to flip a pyramid, especially one that's been covered in millennia of dust, but it's got to be worth a try, right?

Start with some different questions about your work.

Which bits do you enjoy?

Do you actually enjoy any of them? Or do you enjoy the concept of them?

Are there skills and components to the job you wish you had?

Once you've broken it down once, do it again. Look inside each component to find that fundamental kernel of enjoyment. For me as an accountant, financial modelling was something I enjoyed a lot but I would say it's the problem solving and the programming side of it that I enjoy the most. My enjoyment has nothing to do with building profit and loss accounts and deciding on appropriate inputs, it instead has everything to do with solving a puzzle and doing it through creating infallible logic.

"You're such a geek it's untrue."

Taking the time to investigate your current position and what brings you real happiness will help you uncover what you should be looking for in the future if and when you do consider mixing things up.

GOOD

Figuring out what you actually like is a good start, but if you want to make a move, or change direction in your career, regardless of whether it is a big change or a small change, you'll probably need to have some transferable skills to help you on your way.

You need to know what you are good at!

"Nothing!"

Starting from scratch isn't out of the question, but then you will need to consider what can be achieved by starting again and in what time frame, which we'll discuss soon.

This is about feedback and how others view your work and successes. It's also about accepting that feedback and not just disagreeing with things you don't like.

I have issues with my confidence. I have issues with my body image. You know this already. I think I'm fat and unattractive. To face my fears around it, I started asking my friends, of both genders, whether they think I am attractive, regardless of whether they personally find me attractive. It's a strange question to ask and it was hard hearing the responses, even when they were positive!

"We're British! We don't compliment people!"

The key part is trusting that the person speaks to you honestly.

If people you trust are saying you're good at something, or that you're actually looking really healthy, you need to take that compliment to heart. Similarly, if people keep saying you need to improve upon a certain area, or that you could probably do with drinking less, it's probably best not to include it in the 'I'm good at this' pile.

I suck at doing this.

"Put 'sucking at things' in the 'I'm good at this' pile."

There are things I consider myself good at that I'm not.

There are things I don't consider myself good at that I am.

I blame him.

"Me?"

There are few where they overlap, but where they overlap it is important to recognise it. The main area I have learned they overlap for me is in my presentation skills – particularly verbal, but also written. I am a good talker, listener and communicator. I can connect the dots.

You've made it five chapters into this book and you're still reading, right?

I can't be that bad at it!

Can I?

Don't answer that.

"Are you talking to me?"

REAL

The final part of reflection is to understand what is realistic.

Back when you were a blank slate you had a lot more options available to you. Not only because you had no previous skills but also because you had the time ahead of you to develop into what you wanted to become.

This is where we can bring in some more training and talk about sunk cost.

"You're a sunk cost!"

A sunk cost is simply a cost that has already been incurred and cannot be recovered.

Our training to become a qualified lawyer or accountant may have taken us upwards of ten years to complete. Does moving away from this field mean those ten years are wasted?

No, not really.

But also, yes.

Over a training contract and the work up until qualification you will have gained a lot of transferable skills. These could include things like people management, understanding of financial statements, how to document properly, managing corporate risk and governance etc. These skills will be with you always, if you continue to use them every so often.

However, the flip side is also true.

Every career path will involve things related to that specific industry. If you want to move from finance to programming, or to marketing, your knowledge of financial statements won't help you in the day job. It may help you as you move towards the top of an organisation in that industry, maybe as part of a leadership role, but it won't help you with skills such as running a successful social media campaign, or how to architect a technology stack.

Believe me.

I've tried!

The scary thing about starting my work on public speaking, running my website and even writing this book was that I was responsible for everything. I was the only one who could do it and the only person I could rely upon. I taught myself everything about it.

> *"That's why everything is so rough around the edges!"*

This is where understanding what you can realistically achieve becomes very important. What compromises are you willing to make along the way?

A typical decision, and one I admit I have made, is to seek a job you don't like in an industry you do like – e.g. becoming a financial accountant in a premier league football club.

> *"Trying to open this book up to a wider audience? You're too late!"*

This is where you stick with your qualification and try to utilise it similarly in an industry you have an interest in. Doing this can be very rewarding; but it can also lead to unhappiness.

The key as always is to consider yourself and your opportunities ahead of time.

You are always better to make a proactive decision than a reactive decision. You should move somewhere because you want to move there, rather than move somewhere because you don't like where you are.

Regretting Regretting

BLOT

With all decisions, it is possible that we get them wrong.

I've fucked up a lot of decisions.

I've fucked up my life.

The thing with fuck-ups is that the world around you and those on the outside might not even see your choices and actions as fuck-ups.

They'll likely just see it as a decision you made.

In fact, they'll probably not even care about the decision-making process at all and in time will have forgotten what even happened.

They probably won't even remember you.

"This is where I come in. I'm never going to let you forget about those decisions. I'm never going to let you forget mistakes. You're going to remember them until you die. When gasping for your last breath, the last thing you'll think about is how you spoke to that stranger on the tube in London when you were in your twenties."

Yep.

They're an absolute arsehole when it comes to regret and shame. The reason they're such an arsehole is because it's their job. They exist to protect us. There was something painful about the events that led to this shame and regret, and they don't want to see it happen again. They're looking out for us in the only way they can, by reminding us of mistakes we made so we can avoid the same mistake again.

"Always gonna bring it up.
Always gonna drag you down.
Always gonna run aground and subvert you.
Always gonna ask you 'why?'
Always gonna make you cry.
Always gonna tell you lies and hurt you."

VAIN

Shame and regret are two emotions that are entirely personal.

You cannot feel shame for someone else.

You cannot feel regret for someone else.

We say things like 'I feel embarrassed for them', but what we mean is that if we were in that situation, we would feel the embarrassment. We're not embarrassed.

Similarly, we can't feel regret for someone else. We can feel sadness for them and the regret they feel. We can feel remorse for their loss as the result of a bad decision. We cannot feel their regret.

These two feelings are on you.

You cannot easily seek help with these feelings, so you must learn to address them and come to terms with them yourself.

This is a lot easier said than done.

I carry a lot of shame and a lot of regret. I am ashamed of almost everything I have done and regret almost every decision I have made. I carry this with me always. It is a burden that I cannot share and one that I work on constantly with the hope that it diminishes over time.

It sucks.

It really does.

I will discuss my shame and regret more later, but for now, know that I am speaking from a place of carrying a lot of it.

I am going to try and share how I approach my shame and regret and how I continue, despite feeling like a constant failure in every aspect of my life. I fight to become more comfortable in myself.

PICK

So how do I address my shame and regret?

It would be easy to say that I don't address it at all.

I simply ignore it and I move on.

> *"Like I'm going to allow that to happen. Wouldn't want a repeat of any of this now, would we?"*

I don't.

Ignorance is bliss, but only for the ignorant.

If it was possible to ignore these feelings, then it would certainly be an option. If you're able to detach these memories and not replay them over in your head, great, do it. You'll find peace quickly but won't necessarily grow from it!

My biggest issue is I don't want to be ignorant. I'd love some bliss, but at the expense of ignorance? No, thank you. I have always wanted to understand 'why?' and I imagine many of you are the same. Why did I make that decision? Why did it result in this? Why can't I let it go? I like facing into the pain because it allows me to grow and become more resilient.

I address my memories and feelings by allowing myself time to consider them. I simply limit that time.

Reflection is a good. Rumination is a bad.

> *"That's a quote I'd be happy to be remembered for. Put that in the blurb somewhere."*

It's a fine line.

When I start reflecting on a decision, or an action, or something that happened, I try not to allow myself to run over it repeatedly. I write down each of the major points I'm considering and each of the main pains I am feeling.

A spider diagram of questions, emotions and thoughts spreads forth across the page.

Once there is nothing left to add, I put it away. When I find myself reflecting on the same decision, action or occurrence, I look at that same diagram and see if there is something new to add to it or if I am just re-treading old ground.

What I find is that after a few views of the scribbles and scrawls, there is nothing more to add and I stop needing to reflect on it. Simply knowing I've already 'worried enough' about it makes me worry less.

The good thing about these diagrams is they can interconnect, and you can begin to see common themes emerging from them.

One of the biggest revelations I had from my diagrams was that a lot of my shame and regret came from disappointing my parents, particularly my dad.

When I considered this further and spent the time reflecting, I realised it was because when I was young, my dad was working incredibly hard and was often working away during the week. When I finally had the chance to see him on weekends, I wanted him to want to spend time with me, so constantly sought his attention and affection.

From realising this, I now have a much closer and much more rewarding relationship with my dad than ever before. It is something I am proud to have worked on and built upon. Even though I'm not the successful accountant I was supposed to be, and I've failed more times than I can count, I hope he is proud of what I have achieved.

> *"Everyone fails at who they're supposed to be. The measure of a person is how well they succeed at being who they are."*

Are you being nice to me for a change?

> *"No. I'm just quoting Avengers: Endgame."*

TAKE

All the time you spend reflecting and getting to know yourself is done with a single purpose: to accept yourself, your decisions and to allow you to find happiness in yourself.

We all make mistakes along the way.

We all have things we regret and feel shame about.

A lot of shame and regret comes from what other people may or may not think about us and the decisions we have made.

> *"You're thinking about how the Partner you worked for over a decade ago probably sees you as a complete failure and has no respect for you."*

By finding acceptance in ourselves and in our decisions, we can leave behind the opinions of others. Who cares what they think? You don't need their approval. You don't need a carefully written and well-articulated reason for making your decisions. You just need to find happiness in those decisions.

If this means you probably shouldn't have signed a training contract to become an accountant, spent six to seven years in practice, moved to industry and then muddled your way along a career always trying to replicate what it was like in practice without being in practice then so be it.

> *"Weirdly specific, but okay. You got some regrets there, buddy?"*

Be happy.

Learn from your mistakes.

And become a better you.

Do Not Blame Past You

KIDS

Ever been told you are a completely different person when drunk?

> *"Wait till the morning. I'll remind you!"*

Drunk Andy always seems to look after Hungover Andy quite well.

He always makes sure to drink water, eat some carbs and take some painkillers before going to sleep.

Drunk Andy never used to be like this. When Drunk Andy was younger, he was awful. He just kept drinking and drinking and made Hungover Andy into an awful person to be around.

> *"You're pretty awful to be around now, even when you're not drunk."*

It's amazing how we can look back on ourselves and believe we've always been the same. I like adding adjectives to differentiate the various versions of myself. We are different people at different points in our lives. What matters to you as a child is different from what matters to you as a teenager, which again is totally different to what matters to you whilst at university. And so on.

Why do we stop recognising this when we become an adult and start working? We seem to believe that we stop growing up and changing, as if once we hit 'adult' that's it.

> *"It is. All that follows is picket fences, fine china and a hefty dose of anxiety."*

Being an adult is more than feeling exhausted every hour of the day, wishing you hadn't made plans and wondering why your back is hurting again.

> *"My fondest memory of being 'young' is not feeling exhausted all the time."*

Being an adult is an evolution process.

Not in the way that humans are just monkeys with anxiety!

There is a level of personal growth and development.

There is a lot going on and sometimes it's hard to see it whilst you're living it. Everything about you will likely change over time. The least worrying thing about it will be the grey hairs!

> *"It's when you get grey hairs not on your head that's the biggest shock!"*

Young Andy was naive.

> *"He was also an absolute arsehole!"*

He believed that he could achieve anything. He didn't consider the downside risk of decisions and just thought he'd land on his feet. He didn't consider the help of others because he believed he was strong enough alone.

Young Andy was wrong.

Young Andy made bad decisions.

Present Andy now deals with being handed a sack full of hungry and angry kittens who haven't seen the light of day in a while.

> *"Kind of similar to how the millennial generation needs to deal with the climate change problem, the pension deficit problem and all the rest handed over by Boomers."*

Shots fired!

Regret and shame of Young Andy's actions would be natural, but at the same time, he was a different person with different experiences. He didn't know what would happen as a result of his decisions. He made those decisions based on his available information and experiences at the time.

Young Andy didn't do anything wrong.

"Didn't he?"

REAP

We don't know what the outcome of our decisions will be ahead of time. We aren't handed a walkthrough for life, showing us where to find elixirs and other hidden treasures along the way.

We reap what we sow and it's important that we both realise and accept it.

Even though I live with Past Andy's decisions, I must accept that he made those decisions in good faith, believing they were right for him and what he was working towards at the time. Past Andy must have put in some thought regardless of how bad the consequences might be for Present Andy.

The results may have been different to what he believed would happen, but he couldn't have known that at the time. Future Andy won't be able to hold a grudge against Present Andy for writing all this shit down and publishing it in a book. Future Andy will just have to deal with it.

"Sucker."

If Present Andy is stuck with Past Andy's decisions and Future Andy can't judge Present Andy, and the opinions of other people aren't important, and two trains are travelling at sixty miles per hour towards one another, and an apple is dropped at a forty degree angle from one train, who or what really matters?

> *"You really just throwing a bad geometry puzzle in?*
> *Only a handful of people will laugh."*

You.

You matter.

Focus on you.

Focus on now.

The past is written.

The future is unwritten.

Focus on the now and what is right for you right now. If that means changing careers or trying to find new meaning from life, then do it. If it means 'sticking to the knitting' and keeping going despite how tough it is, then do it. If it means writing a book about all your many failures in some attempt to bring atonement and meaning to the pain and suffering you've been through over the past few years that is objectively nowhere near as bad as what other people struggle with every day all over the world, then do it.

> *"Again, weirdly specific, buddy. You okay?"*

Be selfish and look after yourself.

It really is that simple.

KNOW

Is it really that simple?

Yes.

No.

Sometimes.

"You don't do it!"

You need to put yourself first and you need to listen to what you are feeling. You need to reflect on what has happened and where you want to go, without obsession and rumination. You want to make it all make sense in some grand design.

Sadly, it's not that easy.

Nothing is.

It has taken me three years of therapy, working almost weekly with the same therapist, and I only feel like I had my first real breakthrough last week. It was incredible. People may say it's money wasted since it took so long, but to me it is the best money I have ever spent. It has allowed me to reflect on my life honestly, consider where I am in the world and see how the grand tapestry of my existence is all woven together.

"And frayed all over? It's so poetic, you should write a book!"

The most important lesson of this chapter and probably of this whole book is to get to know yourself. Once you know yourself and can understand yourself, why you made those decisions in the past and what you genuinely want to see in your future, then life will become a lot simpler and a lot easier.

I know I'm not an accountant in my heart.

I don't enjoy it.

I'm good at it and I will continue to do it for as long as I need to, but I don't think I'll ever really get excited over it.

"Who does?!"

My passion lies elsewhere.

I will live with the decisions I made that got me to where I am; but now I'm pivoting.

It's scary, I'm doing it alone, but it'll be better for me in the long run.

I'll find my passion and I hope my experiences help you find yours!

TRAP

SIX

RISK, REWARD, REDUNDANCY AND REPETITION

Closed Doors, Opened Windows and Hurricane Glass

ENVY

Humanity is community.

There are almost eight billion of us on our little blue planet, all part of the same species, all with the same fundamental biology. With so many of us it's easy to see why we compare ourselves so easily.

Sometimes this comparison is through experience, other times through title and sometimes even worth. We do this to seek our place in the world and to understand where we are in our lives.

We do it to discover belonging!

In previous chapters I have spoken about how you are unique and how you should embrace your individuality. If you believe any of my ramblings

"Unlikely."

then you should also, hopefully, be able to extrapolate this to understand why you cannot possibly compare yourself to anyone else. There are too many variables, too many differences, too many nuances to even be able to liken yourself to someone else. There may be similarities, but not enough to make a worthwhile comparison.

Unfortunately, comparison is natural!

We all do it!

"She's skinnier than I am. He's taller than me. They've got a bigger house than us. Their family is so well off. His life sounds so exciting. She's got a girlfriend now."

However,

"Why do you always do this?!"

I do not support comparison. We can't reasonably compare ourselves to one another. I appreciate why we do and why we want to; I just believe accepting ourselves first is more important.

I think we should be proud of our individuality and proud of who we are.

This chapter is about acceptance. Accept yourself. Accept your weaknesses. Accept your strengths. Accept who you are. Accept where you are in life.

"It's not what I wanted. It's not what I planned. It's not where I thought I'd be. It's just where I am."

HATE

Comparison is flawed.

We've already talked about how each of us is unique and cannot reasonably be compared. Even with simplifications, it is near impossible to separate the nature and the nurture between people.

The other major flaw with comparison is that it aims to put people on an axis.

"Excuse me? What?"

When you are comparing anything, the aim is to try and say that 'this person is at position X' and 'this person is at position Y'. This is okay, until you try to assert the relative positions of X and Y.

This is where comparison fails.

At this point, you are now deciding a winner or a loser.

"Are you trying to make your two degrees in mathematics useful?"

Start simply: your friend from work got promoted and you didn't. You see their new salary and your current salary. They are now earning more than you.

"Just the words 'more than' sound bitter!"

Go a step further.

Consider the same person. They have just bought a new house and you look at the price.

"Thanks, Zoopla!"

Suddenly you compare it to your house – you know, the one you've been happy with for years?

Does it make you feel any different? Are they more successful than you? Do they have more money than you? Does it make them happier?

When I bought my first house, I was incredibly lucky. I come from a wealthy family. It's a fact. I can't hide it. I am ashamed of it. That's for me to accept. The privilege provides me with the opportunity to do things many others cannot.

"Like write a book?"

I try not to talk about it.

The deposit I was able to raise was significantly more than that which others at a similar point in their career would have accumulated. The house I was able to purchase was above and beyond what many would aspire to at that point in their lives. Everyone who visited immediately said, 'This is amazing, you've done so well for yourself.'

"No, you hadn't!"

I hadn't.

I went into full denial mode: 'It wasn't me that afforded it.' I was constantly defending the position that I shouldn't be compared to them. I didn't want them to feel that they were in a worse position under any circumstances. I would likewise measure myself against what they were achieving without my family and would feel worse.

I felt that none of my success was my own.

"Success?"

The very thought of comparison bothers me.

I am ashamed of my privilege, despite all the positives it has brought to my life. One of my closest and dearest friends said when visiting my flat, 'So this is how the other half live.' I believed that all our years of friendship would allow them to see beyond such things and view us as equals. However, in that moment, all that mattered was money.

It was painful and still haunts me.

As a counterpoint, one of the most joyous moments in my life was back at college when I told some friends that I was going to collect my A Level results the next day and they were surprised I was even at college. They valued me as me and didn't even know of my education.

I would encourage you to stop looking at similarities and differences as all it does is lead to envy and hate.

> *"Which lead to suffering and the dark side of mental health..."*

LAUD

So, what should we do?

We're always going to see the successes of other people around us.

> *"Thanks, LinkedIn. Thanks, Facebook. Thanks, Twitter. Thanks, Instagram. You make my job of making Andy feel miserable so easy!"*

Well, just as you should be happy in yourself and where you are, you should be happy for those people.

See their success and praise them. See their achievements and be happy for them. Whatever they have achieved, it's theirs.

Similarly, whatever you achieve, you should be happy in also.

I still find it hard to accept my privilege. I still find it hard to separate what I have achieved and what I have achieved because of my family. It's tough. I am still trying to find my happiness and acceptance and still find it hard to praise myself.

All I can ask is that as you try to learn to love and accept yourself, you also learn to love and praise those around you.

Let go of the rulers.

Let go of the tape measures.

Let go of your basic instincts to compare.

Just be happy.

Data-Driven Decisions

DIRT

At some point in your life, or your career, or if I'm honest, in anything, you'll be presented with opportunities that make you consider how they will impact your life.

Sometimes it'll be a push.

This could be in the form of 'I'm fed up and need a change' or 'being made redundant'.

> *"These things always seem to happen during your thirties."*

Other times it'll be a pull such as 'I want you to come and work for me' or 'We want to promote you'.

When these opportunities appear, treat them how you would treat an opportunity that arose for a client or a friend.

"Be jealous and envious, then try to subvert their position and make yours stronger?"

If a client came to you and asked whether they should do something – e.g. acquire a company – you wouldn't just say yes or no. You'd do research. You'd look at facts. You'd see if there was any alignment or synergies that could be gained.

Do the same with your own decisions.

Maybe don't write a twenty-page document speculatively, just think about it similarly.

"How many hours did we lose writing documents that led to nothing?"

I am someone who will always offer help. People regularly come to me asking questions. When I am asked for advice there is a typical list of things that I consider.

Work through these questions by yourself and then talk through your responses with someone else, ideally someone unconnected to the decision but who cares about you and understands the broader context of the decision!

Hell, talk it through with multiple people!

Just base your decisions on facts rather than feels.

HERE

I am going to use an example that many of us will have experienced at one point in our careers to keep this as open as possible.

"Famous last words."

Work is shit. I'm fed up. Life is boring. Something needs to change.

How many of you have felt like this?

"They can't answer you!"

It's pretty bad when you get here.

You know something needs to change but you don't know what.

Well, this is my take on it all.

This is from someone who has pivoted more times than he'd like to admit and failed more times than he can count.

Let's start here: you know you need to change something but don't know what. Let's focus down on changing your job.

I am a firm believer that logistics will always find a way. Distance, money, time and all the other 'Hows' will be figured out once you know the 'Whats' that have come from your 'Whys'.

At this point you should focus on 'Whats'.

What do you want to do? What is your current job not giving you that you want? What do you care about?

Would changing jobs stop you from finishing a qualification? Many companies pay for your study towards qualifications, but if changing jobs now makes you need to stop your studies – or worse, repay back what has been spent – you need to consider these costs.

Would changing jobs lead to a promotion? Or even a demotion? Does the status of a new role matter to you?

On a very fundamental level, what about the money? Would your net disposable income change? Don't think about total figure or long-term value; stay in the here and now. Would your quality of life increase or decrease as a result of this move?

If you are going to interviews, ask the questions that matter to you. If you are lacking life balance, then you need to be asking about it. If you are lacking money, then you need to ask about it. What about the commute and your time lost if this changes?

This is your time to ask the questions that matter to you!

I've taken a new tack when interviewing people and when being interviewed.

> *"Interviews are always two-way."*

I have started asking questions such as 'When was the last time you cried and why?', 'What is the one thing that you wouldn't want your boss or a client to know about you?' and 'If an employee came to you and said they were suicidal, what would you do?'

> *"These are brutal questions. I don't want to work for you!"*

I don't ask these to be awkward.

Well, maybe a little.

I ask these questions because I want to know how emotionally aware the people are and to see how open they are. If people aren't willing to talk about their pain, or consider how to support others in pain, then are they people I want to work with?

What matters to me is if someone is working with me, I want them to be able to treat me as a friend and know they can come to me with anything. I want to not only support their career growth, but also support their personal growth.

Also, would I really want someone by my side who is an emotionless, unfeeling, corporate monster?

"Just like you were."

ELSE

You've figured out the 'What' of the situation and now need to start thinking about 'Who'.

Clearly this decision will impact your life but who else around you will it also affect?

There are the obvious people any decision will affect like children, husbands, wives, girlfriends, boyfriends, other immediate family and pets. If you are cohabiting in any sense of the word, your decisions may well impact those around you and you should be considerate of what could happen to those people too.

There are the slightly less obvious, including your friends and extended family. If you are moving, changing hours, or doing something new, will your relationship with any of them change at all? Will you be able to still go to events together or hang out in the same way? Will people who care about you from further away still be able to do that?

Will you still be able to socialise as you do currently, or will that change? Will you lose access to your friends?

Finally, there are the peripheries. These are people such as colleagues, who you spend a lot of time with, but ultimately who owe you nothing and vice versa. Your decision to change jobs might create a gap in your team or might leave someone who works for you without a mentor to oversee them. You might feel an obligation to them, but you shouldn't let them, or their situation, determine your life.

Fundamentally, any decision is yours. You shouldn't hold yourself back for anyone else. Those that matter will accept your decision and support you regardless of their opinions. Those that don't matter will fade away.

"Fuck 'em."

You will quickly realise who are your real friends. You will quickly understand who really cares about you.

Make your decisions for you and you alone.

LUST

We all have an image in our minds about what our future self should look like and what our future self should be doing.

Being comfortable in who you are is incredibly important; by finding that comfort in your present self, you should also seek comfort for your future self.

What do you honestly see in your future?

"Going to the pub with my best friend, people watching for hours, drinking far too much cider, putting the world right and laughing till our cheeks hurt."

If your image is one of leadership, partnership or being an expert in a field, how does this change drive you towards that? If your image is one of family and having a positive life balance, being able to relax without picking up e-mails on a weeknight or weekend, how does this change drive you towards that?

The hardest part of all of this is knowing where you want to go.

Knowing the destination isn't important.

Knowing the direction is.

Don't worry about where you'll end up, nor about how you'll get there.

Just have an idea.

FEAR

With all decisions there is fear.

Life now is firmly pushed towards living with a fear of missing out. 'FOMO' is everywhere. We have information available at our fingertips. We can be contacted instantaneously all over the globe. We have access to so much information that it can be completely overwhelming.

"Thanks for helping me ruin Andy's mental health social media. Couldn't do it without you!"

Simplify.

You're looking at changing jobs, or maybe moving to a new house, maybe even both! What are you afraid of happening? Is that fear rational or even relevant?

The first and most natural fear is if it's the right decision. You can internally debate about whether action or inaction is the correct decision, but you'll never truly know unless you act.

> *"The grass may always be greener but sitting on a fence post is a literal pain in the ass."*

There may also be a fear of embarrassment. People might think it's a bad decision or might think you're throwing away an opportunity. Really though, their opinions don't matter. It's all about you and what is right for you.

There is a natural fear of failure. Our world has made it a lot easier to say no than to say yes.

> *"Swiping left and never knowing is easier than swiping right, trying and failing."*

It's always much easier to just keep going than it is to embrace change. Failure is scary. But if you are denying yourself something from fear, then that is a failure in itself.

There is always a risk of pain.

Pain hurts.

We naturally try to avoid it.

Pain also makes us human. Pain makes us feel. Pain helps us grow. Pain makes us realise what is important.

Stepping out of your comfort zone and embracing a little bit of fear is healthy and should give you the confidence you need to make change happen.

MISS

You've faced into the fear of the decision, but it's important to consider a few final things. Fear is a natural part of decision making, but let's take a quick moment and catastrophise. I advise people not to do this time and time again, but here I'm saying feel it for a moment, just a brief moment.

What is the worst that can happen?

> *"If it doesn't involve spontaneous volcanoes erupting underneath you then it's probably not the worst."*

Let's be realistic about it though.

Let's consider it.

If it's a decision about moving job or moving location what is the actual worst that can happen? If you're moving job, you're still in a job. The logistics might change, but you still have a job. You can always find another new job!

The worst that can happen is likely something out of your control. A miscommunication. A missed appointment. A mistake. But as we've talked about before, focus your energy on things you can control, not on things you can't.

Spend your spoons wisely.

> *"No! Why haven't you dropped these yet?"*

You could lose your new job. That's a possibility. But you just convinced someone to offer you a job, so you can probably do it again. Equally, you could always apply back to your old company; they know you already and if you have kept a healthy relationship there and not burned every bridge then you can hopefully speak honestly to them!

Catastrophise in moderation.

BOLT

However, it's important to fully appreciate everything about your decision.

If everything does go up in flames, what are you going to do?

You join a firm and within a few weeks it's closed due to some scandal or something.

> *"Maybe an accounting scandal? They're pretty common, come to think of it."*

This is completely out of your control. Completely unpredictable. You can do absolutely nothing about it, so there is simply no point worrying about it.

But what if?

What is your fallback?

Sometimes this is knowing your skill set or having a recognised qualification. I personally know full well I could fall back into being a 'boring, run of the mill accountant' if it was necessary.

"Death is likely the preferable option."

I don't want to, but I know it is a backup!

I equally know that if my world comes crumbling down around me again that I will always have my family. They've supported me through the worst of times. I believe they will continue to do the same, time and time again.

I also know I have my friends who care about me and my wellbeing. Whilst they may not be able to offer me a job or put a roof over my head, I know they'll stand by me and help in whatever way they can. They've stood by me through a lot so far and I trust them to do it again.

I always want to fail myself. I believe that I need to fail by myself to grow as a person. I need to feel that pain, accept it and keep going.

Knowing that I have backup allows me to fail.

It has allowed me to fail over and over again.

It allows me to keep failing!

There are very few people who will support you and who care for you in a completely selfless way. Know who those people are and then never ever let them go. They are the people who will be there for you when things go bad. They will be there for life.

Treasure them always.

Scooby-Doo

RUSH

Things can and do go wrong.

Nothing is ever as smooth as you imagine.

When things go wrong though, it's important not to immediately go into fight or flight or fright.

"Or fuck?"

Human nature will be insisting that you respond immediately and that you jump to action.

Don't.

When we are like this, our judgement is impaired. All the adrenaline surging through us makes us want to act immediately.

This is a push response, and push responses lead us to make less beneficial and positive decisions overall. Slow down. Your heart will be racing, your head will be spinning; take your time and think things through.

Easier said than done, I know!

I was working with a client during the early days of my independent consultancy. They'd asked me to go on payroll for them and I was happy to oblige. I had completed my initial review of the company and uncovered some things that I really wasn't comfortable with.

"Who knew you had a soul!"

Everyone in the organisation knew there was something wrong, but the people at the top weren't listening. I felt something had to be done. Something needed to be changed. So, I did what any self-righteous, over committed and enthusiastic youngster would do and I marched into the Managing Director's office and reported my findings, all written and documented clearly, presenting clear evidence to show the 'corruption' throughout the organisation.

The next day, I was 'fired'.

I knew it was coming. If I'm honest with myself, I'd engineered it. I had realised that I cared more about the wellbeing and happiness of the employees and the customers than I did about the money I was receiving. I fell on my sword for the greater good.

I was a martyr.

Even though I knew it was coming, it didn't stop me from having the palpitations, the nausea and the fear.

I didn't follow my own guidance here.

I lashed back.

Grandiose threats, legal advice and several heated conversations later, I was busy signing a severance agreement. Whilst I had protected my financial position and what mattered in the immediate term, my moral position was compromised. It haunts me to this day that I made this decision.

Clearly, I can't say much more, but I am glad to see that changes have been made at the company.

"Onwards and upwards."

Learn to slow things down ahead of making decisions. You'll never know at the time what decisions will stay with you throughout your life, so take the time to consider them all in earnest so you can live at peace with them.

BODY

Failure is human.

Failure happens to us all.

"Some more than others!"

When we fail it can feel all-encompassing. It can consume us. We can even believe we've failed when we haven't. We put such expectation on ourselves to be successful that we can see anything less than perfection as failure.

Look at online dating!

"What? Where are you going with this?"

As someone who was in a couple for the previous eleven or so years, I was new to online dating. I was forced into it. I have since given up on it. The ease of swiping left and right ruins the fun of what dating and finding someone to fall in love with means to me. I would rather find friendship first and build upon that. As I said in the first chapter, turning a true friendship into real romance can yield the absolute greatest of results and that is what I will continue to search for.

I say this next part from real experience: you look at between one and nine pictures and up to five hundred characters about someone and must decide whether they are worth meeting.

> *"Assuming there even is more than one picture, that they've written a bio and that they're not a catfish."*

The issue is that you can find faults in this tiny window into a person's life. You then extrapolate these tiny imperfections into huge character flaws and suddenly someone who could be your soulmate has been discounted because of that one little detail.

Here are a few paraphrased examples of comments that were made during my brief exploration of online dating: 'Why would you have a picture of you and your friend's child on your Instagram? It must be your child and therefore you're a filthy cheat', 'How tall are you? Height is all-important and if you don't agree it's an attack on my beliefs', 'Why would I want to meet you? I don't know you', 'You're wearing a t-shirt about video games, you must only play FIFA and eat pizza in squalid living conditions', 'You don't play an instrument and I only want someone who plays an instrument to share music with me'.

I give up!

> *"Forever alone."*

No matter what, we find failure in those around us and then we find failure in ourselves.

We start believing that there is no point in it. We start closing off and denying ourselves the excitement that comes with getting to know people and learning about them organically.

When I met my ex-wife, or any of my ex-girlfriends or whatever title you want to put on them, I didn't really know anything about them. There was a thrill in finding out more and uncovering little parts of their personality. Sometimes it turns out to be worthwhile, sometimes it doesn't; but it's that joint and shared discovery that makes it enjoyable and ultimately worthwhile.

The issue nowadays is that it's a time investment.

A time investment followed by a failure hurts a lot. Not only have we failed, but we've spent time, our precious and limited time, our precious and ever diminishing spoons, on something and someone else and nothing good has come from it.

What's the point?

As always, failure makes us human.

We would never have achieved anything in science if the first experiment had given us the result we expected. We would never have discovered other countries or continents if we had just turned around as soon as we hit stormy skies and rough waters.

Failure is part of us.

Love it.

Laugh about it.

Embrace it.

READ

Some famous bloke once said that repetition is insanity.

> *"You're fucking hopeless, stop trying to be cool and pretend you don't know this! It was Albert Einstein. He said, 'The definition of insanity is doing the same thing over and over again and expecting a different result'."*

It is true though.

Learning from failure is important. If you don't learn from your mistakes, or the mistakes of those around you, then you'll never grow as an individual and are destined to repeat them.

I hated history at school. At the time it seemed pointless studying the past when there were new things to be discovered in the present. I craved new knowledge and not old teachings.

> *"Whether it warrants an entire subject to be taught at school is a different matter."*

I now know differently. Learning from mistakes is important. Learning from our past is important. There are many ways to learn from failure. The most common is to change your response the next time the same situation arises.

This is the principle behind cognitive behavioural therapy (CBT).[16]

> *"Please don't."*

---

[16] www.nhs.uk/conditions/cognitive-behavioural-therapy-cbt Accessed on 30/08/19

CBT is about learning to recognise your reactions to stimuli and to then change them. I personally hate CBT. If I could change how I thought, don't you think I'd have done it already!

> *"Genuinely, if you need help, CBT is a valid approach. Don't let Andy dissuade you from it! It may not work on me, but it could work on your version of me."*

This is one of the ways that health services help with mental health, anxiety, stress and any other learned response.

It does work.

I just don't like it.

In the simplest case: What was your failure? What decision caused your failure? If you are put in a similar situation again, can you respond differently? The hard part is knowing the truth underlying it all. You'll have several opinions on what it is but distilling it down to the root cause will be tough.

I cannot speak as an expert here as I am still failing every day. I fail at everything. You'd think I'd be good at it by now. I'm not.

I am still learning myself!

The point is that I'm conscious about being crap at learning from mistakes. I know that I know nothing about it. I keep trying and I keep learning. Trying once and giving up is as pointless as never trying at all.

> *"Always try everything twice! You're probably drunk the first time!"*

Keep going and keep learning.

OPEN

Whatever happens, you shouldn't be ashamed of your failures.

Many people will try to hide them. Many people won't even acknowledge they exist.

Failure is human, so showing your failures shows you are more than just a mindless, work-driven automaton.

Working with and in start-up companies is amazing for this and you get used to writing about, talking about and ultimately succeeding in your failures. The good thing about failures is they often come with a great story.

And I love telling a good story!

"Here we go again."

I was once asked about one of the companies I worked with that had unfortunately ceased trading due to shareholder disputes. I spoke as honestly as I could about it. The person I was speaking to was so impressed with how openly I responded about my failures that I was offered a job on the spot.

They didn't want someone who could only be there in the good times and didn't know how to deal with the bad times. They didn't want a 'yes man'. They wanted someone who had got their hands dirty, who had seen the messy and gritty side of business and who was willing to stand up for what they believe in.

I didn't accept the offer.

"You're an idiot."

The reason?

Mostly because accepting such a job offer would have been a failure to myself and what I was working towards at the time.

Failure builds character.

As long as you learn from it, you will be a better person with a long list of failures behind you than you ever will be if all you've known is success.

Plus.

Success is really boring.

Where's the story? Where's the drama? Where's the romance?

Life is a story and if it's boring no one will want to listen. Why are you reading this book after all? To hear about how well I've done? No. You're here because either I know you and have bullied you into buying and reading it, or your interest has been piqued by the rollercoaster ride that is my life and want to see if you can learn something from it.

I'm not saying go out there and fail on purpose. That would just be stupid.

"You are pretty stupid."

I'm saying go out there and roll the dice.

Life is too short!

Rabbit Holes and Through the Looking Glass

ECHO

How often do you sit at home after a long day at work wondering about how things could have gone differently?

How often do you think about what happened in the past and how your life could be completely different now if only for that one decision you made back then?

How often does this process start spiralling out of control and you start reliving the pain of the past?

"Every. Fucking. Day. Every. Fucking. Time."

Looking back is natural. We are the sum of our experiences and hopefully a little more. Reflecting on these experiences is normal and helps us ground ourselves in the present.

The problem is when we let them consume us. When the hypothetical starts taking precedence over the real, you're thinking about them too much.

The issue about hypotheticals is that you cannot ever consider all probabilities and possibilities. You could make one decision and then suddenly what you think would be a natural follow-on could be completely different.

It is all about moderation and acceptance.

"Like ninety percent of this book! You know you're repeating yourself?"

You cannot change the past. Flux Capacitors are not real. Past You made decisions that were right for Past You at the time.

You need to accept this.

Remember it, but don't ruminate on it!

NOTE

This is a habit I got into when my very first girlfriend broke up with me.

> *"Isn't it amazing how much you're talking about the failures of your love life alongside the failures of your career?"*

I didn't understand it.

I couldn't understand it.

We'd spent three years together.

And it was over.

> *"Hey you! You dodged a bullet by dumping Andy! He's a mess!"*

How naive I was to think it was the end of the world when this happened. It's almost funny looking back.

I decided to write down everything that was going around in my head. Whatever time of day. Whatever the situation. I would carry a little book with me, and I would just write down everything that came to mind about her and the breakup.

There is a very cathartic feeling to putting pen to paper.

The scratching of the nib against the grain of the paper. Seeing the ink flow and occasionally blot on the paper as it dries.

"Getting creepy."

It was painful at first, but what I realised was after a while I was writing the same things. The first page was incoherent nonsense. Emotional and angry. As I moved from page to page at varying times of day, I could begin to see patterns emerging.

Eventually, I just got bored of writing the same things. Something would pop into my mind briefly, but then I'd just think to myself: 'It's already in the book so why worry about it again.'

I allowed myself the time I needed to feel the pain, but in doing so I also allowed myself the time I needed to heal.

This works with career decisions too.

I started using little books, typically A6 in size, carrying them round and just writing the worries on my mind. I could tear the pages out if it was something that my mind wasn't repeating, or I could leave them there to carry on if it was something weightier.

This allowed me time to process.

It may feel stupid whilst you're doing it. It may make you feel worse each time you etch the same words into the paper. It will help you in the long run. It will allow you to connect the disconnected and bring method to the madness.

They say time heals all wounds.

It's true.

It does.

VOID

"Did you really think we were going to write a book without mentioning 'Breaking the Stigma'? You wish!"

This chapter is dedicated to all the men out there. It's about me failing as a man.

Men feel. It doesn't often look like it. We hide it away. We are often ashamed of showing our emotions and what they do to us. But we do feel.

Here's some honesty from the period when I was editing this book.

I was in a dark place and I was almost at a point of taking my own life again. Everything was dark. Why? It was the day before I was going to submit my Decree Absolute, the legal document which formally terminates your marriage. I had always told myself, and no one else of course, that once I was finally divorced, I would end my life. I was facing into the realisation that tomorrow I was going to die. Everything was coming to an end and it was overwhelming. Yet it was also oddly peaceful.

At the end of the day I spoke to my best friend. I cried on the phone to her. I didn't quite say what I have written above as I was ashamed and embarrassed about it.

Regardless though.

She talked me down.

Probably without even realising it.

So, I'm going to say what I am going to say in the clearest, rawest and most honest way possible. I am not going to shy away from exposing the pain I felt. Hopefully this will help anyone who reads this to find the strength to do the same if needed. It doesn't make you less of a person to have emotions and to show them. It makes you stronger!

To the women reading this chapter: you may be thinking 'Wow, how sexist' or 'What about the gender gap?', maybe even 'Such toxic masculinity';

"Much wow!"

the chapter will be accessible to you too. Use it how you will. It will be a brief glimpse into what the men in your life may be feeling but not expressing. Under all the bravado and posturing to try and be 'alpha', there is often just some guy underneath struggling to be who he truly wants to be.

I hope that in saying all of this, everyone – men and women alike – will feel more comfortable talking openly about what is truly on their minds.

SEVEN

BREAKING THE STIGMA WHILST CARRYING STIGMATA

The Hell that Is My Life

SUIT

I have always considered myself a failure. Failure is part of who I am and who I will be going forward. Failure defines me. There are times when luck has overcome my ability to fail and I have succeeded despite expectations.

"Better lucky than good, eh?"

I didn't enjoy where I was in my career. I felt I was at a crossroads. I was out of practice, in both senses of the term. I was picking up scraps of work here and there. Nothing substantial. Nothing interesting. Nothing rewarding.

I was constantly asking myself whether I had done the right thing in standing by my morals.

"You did. I wasn't saying it at the time. If you hadn't, I'd have been making you feel even worse."

I questioned the decisions made throughout my career. Should I have stuck it out in practice? Should I have focused more on Business Intelligence? Should I have sacked it off altogether?

"To do what? Write a book?"

I was questioning whether the ten-plus years of my career to date had even meant anything. Sure, I had a wife, a family, a house, a car and a future, but I had no real purpose.

I had always lived in the future.

I was never content in the present.

What was next?

How do I progress my career fastest? How can I push myself up the proverbial ladder? All those decisions seemed futile at this point.

For once my quick quips, sharp wit and astounding charisma

"Easy on there!"

weren't going to be able to bullshit me through these decisions.

I had failed.

My career had no direction.

I had no path to follow.

I was lost.

I was alone.

And I hurt.

WIFE

Then, just when things seemed like they couldn't get any worse.

My wife left me.

It wasn't as quick as that. The death of our relationship was slow and painful and lasted almost two years.

"We are finally divorced now, two years on. Can we start the healing process now?"

It started in the spring of 2017. I felt she was distant. I felt like she was different. Everything felt uneasy.

"Coexisting, Cohabiting Couple seeking Counselling."

She was coming home from a weekend away with her friends and I sent her a text to see when she would be getting into the station to go pick her up. Her reply seemed distant and she didn't want picking up. I asked if she was okay and the reply I got was on the lines of 'We should sit down and talk.'

"Panic! She's cheated on you! She's pregnant! She's got cancer! Panic!"

Fuck.

"Panic! It's all over. She's bringing her new husband over who's going to kill you and swallow your soul. Panic!"

I felt sick.

When we sat down, it was clear there was something deeply troubling her. It looked like something internal, something that was hers and hers alone. Then, in an uncertain tone, again, paraphrased, 'I think I'm a lesbian, not just bisexual.'

"Finish him."

I will spare much of the details here out of respect for her. Needless to say, I knew she was bisexual pretty much since we first met on MySpace.

"Fucking hell. I'm so happy MySpace lost all their data."

I even encouraged her to pursue her first lesbian relationship to be true to herself. A couple of years later we were dating, got married and now we were here, our lives falling apart and eleven years wasted.

"It wasn't wasted, but it felt that way."

The uncertainty in her revelation resulted in six months of torture for us. It was absolute agony. I was fighting for a woman I loved and a marriage I believed in.

She was fighting for herself.

It was a losing battle that I knew I could never win.

But the battle was worse than I could have imagined. Because she was so uncertain of it and also so scared for me and my mental health, no decisions were made and no actions were taken. Everything was left to me. In the end, I was the one who had to say the words, 'It's over. I think we should get a divorce.'

She knew under the law she couldn't ask for one. She knew asking for one could drive me further into my depression. She tried to protect me in a way. It just made things worse.

I cannot describe how much it hurt.

I cannot begin to tell you the pain I still feel now knowing that it was me who said it.

It was consuming. I had to shred one of my beliefs: marriage is for life. Thick and thin. No way out. An everlasting bond saying, 'I've got your back, you've got mine.'

Only my partner didn't have my back.

My partner didn't even have her own back.

What the actual fuck?!

> *"It was messed up. It was really messed up. You needed to do it though. You did. You're better off for it, right? Right?"*

CATS

Losing your wife and ending a marriage or relationship is a deeply painful process that can take a long time.

> *"Two years! Five percent of your life!"*

I am grateful that we didn't have children. It is a saving grace. I can only talk about this as hearsay, but the damage done from a divorce to any children is unquantifiable.

Clearly there can be amicable divorces, like mine and my ex-wife's. Clearly there can be good that comes of it, as it shows everyone is entitled to find themselves and their own happiness.

It's not all doom and gloom.

But here's some fuel for the fire.

We were trying to have children.

We were planning to be parents.

I was planning on being a dad.

That future was now gone.

I had just killed those hypothetical children by asking to end our marriage. Their future ended before it had begun. I murdered the younglings.

"It's a dark way to look at things. I know I said it, but it's extreme in hindsight."

We did have cats though.

Whatever anyone says, my cats were my children. Sky and Roxy – Tamiyo before them – were my children. Knowing that our shared house would need to be sold meant that they would lose their home. I didn't know what my future would hold; all I cared about was finding those cats a loving household so they could have happy outdoor lives.

It was heartbreaking posting on Facebook and asking friends whether anyone could adopt them.

Thankfully, I was lucky.

One of my oldest friends offered to adopt them both. He was considering getting cats anyway and he knew Sky and Roxy well. I think somewhere in it all he just wanted to try and win Roxy over.

I don't think he has yet even after all these years.

Regardless.

I had failed them.

I had failed them all.

BABY

My house and household were falling apart. The person who I would usually seek comfort in wasn't there for me anymore.

I was alone.

I went to the only people who have always been there for me no matter what, my parents.

My dad lovingly refers to me as his 'Number One Son'.

I don't like this. It implies ranking and ordering, even if that ranking is based on the order of our birth. I had failed them as a son, yet they were the only place I could turn.

They had spent countless thousands supporting my ex-wife and me over the years. They took us on numerous holidays, helped fund our wedding, helped us with the deposit for our house, helped us buy cars and helped us by giving us a place to live together before we could buy a house. They cared for us and loved us.

All that money, just as the eleven years of relationship, was wasted.

> *"It wasn't. It didn't feel like it at the time, but it wasn't wasted."*

I had failed them as a son.

Those children I killed that never existed. They were their grandchildren. They would have been their first grandchildren. I killed them. There would never be four generations of our family alive at one time because I had to kill my non-existent children by ending a marriage that I believed in.

I turned to them and as always, they stood by me. They supported me. They lifted me up. I can never thank them enough. May this book be a testament to them and the love they provided during this time.

TEEN

I have two brothers. They are brilliant. They are a lot closer to each other than I am to either of them. There are only two years between them when there are five and seven between them and me respectively.

However, being the eldest, they always looked up to me. Even though they'll never admit it. I was always the first.

"The Number One Son? Sigh."

I set the bar for them and it was often quite high. They always pushed themselves to stand out as younger siblings always do, but they always looked up to who I was and what I was achieving.

"Nothing."

Now though, I wasn't someone worth looking up to. There was nothing in me to follow or aspire towards. They would now be the firsts. They would bring grandchildren into the family. They would have their happy marriages and would lead good lives. My life would be empty.

I was now the one who looked to them as what happiness and success could be. It was a juxtaposition I never thought possible.

It hurt.

They stood by me and supported me. Everyone did. My friends, my family, my colleagues and even strangers. Everyone told me I had done nothing wrong.

"I didn't. I was telling you it was all your fault all along and that you should have seen it coming a mile away."

Thanks for that, inner me. You always know just the right thing to say.

MATE

I was utterly distracted from life. I was distracted with all the pain. There wasn't enough of me left to do what I needed to do, let alone what I wanted to do.

I abandoned my oldest friend's first daughter's naming day ceremony.

> *"That is one hell of a mouthful."*

I was meant to be giving a blessing or speech. I just couldn't do it. How was I meant to wish this newborn a happy and fulfilling life when I felt only sadness and emptiness? I just felt I couldn't ever provide what was expected.

I let other friends down. I stopped going to social events. I became more and more reclusive and introverted as the distractions and decisions were delayed.

I hid away.

I isolated myself.

> *"Good. Good."*

But here's the thing about friends.

Real fucking friends.

Not acquaintances.

Not colleagues.

Real friends.

You know who your real friends are because they're the ones who will text you out of the blue asking how you are. They're the ones you can spend months and even years without seeing and then when you finally meet up, nothing has changed. They'll be there no matter what. Real friends care about you and will always have your back and will never let you down, no matter what!

I know who my best friends are. They're the people who jumped on a train, or in a car, or just turned up on my doorstep to be there.

One example of this is when some of my friends organised an event called 'Justice for Andy'.

It was beautiful.

They all came together, gate-crashed my house, ate food, played board games and drank some beers. It was the nicest of gestures, organised not by the people who I considered my closest friends, but by friends who were relatively new in my life. It was that day I realised these people were real friends and that I never wanted to lose them.

No matter how much happiness I felt during 'Justice for Andy', I quickly lost that feeling. It evaporated when I closed the door behind them.

Back to being alone.

Back to isolation.

MALE

I was a failure in every part of my life.

"Yep."

Regardless of how correct it is, there is an underlying belief that men should be strong, vigilant, robust, alpha-male type leaders who can withstand the pressures of life without emotions getting the better of them.

I felt a complete failure.

I was a complete failure.

I failed at being a man. I couldn't provide for my wife. I felt I couldn't even please her sexually anymore.

I failed as a man.

I was broken.

I needed fixing.

I just didn't know how.

SOUL

Whilst married, I had stopped thinking about the 'I' and only thought about the 'We'. I was no longer defining myself as an individual and was defining myself only as part of a couple. I had given up my individuality willingly.

When I lost the 'We', I didn't know who the 'I' was anymore. What defined Andy?

> *"Who even cares? That guy is a loser."*

I had lost everything in my life over the space of a year and now there was nothing left.

Everything was gone.

There are many stresses in life, some of the biggest being getting married or divorced, losing a loved one, moving to a new house, having a child and being diagnosed or managing an illness. Each of these at once can put significant stress on your life. Too many can push you too far.

Too many can push you to the edge.

I had all of them apart from having a child occur in the space of six months to a year.

I was getting divorced, losing my wife, being forced to move to a new house, all whilst managing my depression.

None of it was my fault.

None of it was my choice.

"Wasn't it?"

I couldn't have chosen anything differently. I couldn't have walked a different path. These were matters I had no choice in.

With nothing left, my depression started consuming me. It consumed all of me. Not just the happiness, the sadness was consumed as well.

I was empty and numb.

HUSK

I became a shell of a human being. I was able to function. I still went to work. I still socialised with friends. I still smiled and laughed. I was just doing it through reflex as it was expected.

"We existed."

I would put my mask on every day. I smiled at Sky and Roxy saying, 'Today is going to be a better day.' It never was. When friends would ask me how things were, I would answer with a smile saying, 'Yeah. Everything is fine. All good. You?'

"Such a liar. So good at it too!"

No one thought any the wiser. Avoidance was key. Don't let on anything because then you don't have to talk about it. You can't show your weaknesses if you don't acknowledge them.

I was rotten inside.

A few cracks showed but not many. I made sure to hide away when I couldn't control it. I still cared about myself, oddly enough. I swore I would never turn to alcohol or drugs during this time and I never did. I know I have an addictive personality and I didn't want to make things worse.

I still don't drink alcohol or take drugs when I'm struggling. It's an honest promise I made and it's an honest promise I will keep.

It's funny looking back. I was doing lots of things right at the time but none of them were done correctly.

I knew I needed to look after myself, so I focused on things I knew I loved like unhealthy food. I knew I needed to have some enjoyment in myself, so I hid inside playing computer games. I knew I needed to keep connected to people, so I carried on working on things I didn't enjoy and that weren't rewarding. I knew I needed rest, so I would spend hours and hours in bed even if I wasn't sleeping.

I started hating my existence.

I wasn't who I thought I was or thought I should be.

> *"Should is a swear word."*

I felt a burden to everyone.

I wanted to end it.

I wanted to end my life.

The Science of Selling Yourself Short

FAKE

Before we cover my downward spiral, it's important to remember that everything I was feeling was my own creation.

> *"It was my creation. You just lived with it. It's my creation. All mine!"*

Taking a step back and looking objectively is incredibly important. If you don't try to see things from an outside perspective, you can get caught in the headlights of self-doubt. If we look at where I was objectively, I was mid-thirties with good career prospects and had a lovely house that would likely sell well, releasing a lot of equity. I was in a position where I would for once in my life be able to follow my own dreams without any hindrance.

That's not a bad place to be.

But I didn't believe it.

And it's not what I was telling myself.

"Nope. You're a fake!"

When I talk about imposter syndrome, it is the feeling that you shouldn't be where you are, that somehow you just got lucky, winged it, and are now in a position you are underqualified or underprepared to be in.

Sound familiar?

Well, here's something that may surprise you. It affects all of us, regardless of our success.

Onto another story.

I love my dad. He is an inspiration to me.

"And he has a story that is worth telling!"

One Sunday evening many years ago, we had just finished Sunday dinner together as a family. It was a pretty rough time for him. He sat at the head of the table and with a tear in his eye, said that he felt he had 'failed in his career'.

What the actual fuck?

This is one of the most successful people I've ever met, if not the most successful person I will ever meet! How on earth can he consider himself a failure at all?

He continued, 'I'm coming to the end of my career and I've never been chief executive of a FTSE100 company.'

"That's hardly failure."

Erm. Okay.

By that measure, at any one time there are only about one hundred successful people and everyone else is a failure.

Seriously?

Skipping forward to the present day, we were sat having breakfast relatively recently one Sunday morning and he says, 'I just can't believe I have this job. It just doesn't feel real.' He continues to describe himself as 'just some Yorkshireman'

"Just another guy?"

who wants to be at home with his wife and family. He carries on: that on a Monday when he gets up to catch the six a.m. train to London, he puts on his suit and his mask and then starts a completely different life.

The fact that he described it as a mask, that it's not really him and that he is just 'some Yorkshireman', made me laugh.

"It's everything we talk about. There's no way it can be true coming from him!"

This is imposter syndrome.

This is what I live with.

In fact, it's probably what most people live with.

We continued the discussion, talking about how both our generations feel the same thing and that the only fundamental difference is that the 'boomer' generation is one of stoicism and reverence, whereas the 'millennial' generation is one of community and communication. It's amazing how different economic climates, different advancements in technology and newly discovered science can have such an impact on the mentality and wellbeing of generations.

Both generations feel like fakes. The boomers are now recruiting and promoting the millennials which means there's respect between them. The millennials are teaching the boomers how to better use technology and communication. It's symbiotic. What it means though is that we can't all be fakes. Everyone in this simplistic example is bringing something the other needs and is rewarded for it.

So even if you feel like a fake, you're not!

"Unless you really are. Then you are a fake."

HUSH

So why do we all feel like fakes in the first place?

"Me?"

Yes. You!

It is our inner voices and inner critics that judge us. They speak to us and compare us to others around us. They don't always listen to what the conscious brain tells them so instead they act on simpler impulses and feelings.

There is no easy silence. You will never truly stop thinking about the comparisons. Sorry. It would be great if you could, but sadly it's not that easy! What you can do is limit the chances your inner critic has to make such comparisons.

"Wait, what? Don't you dare try to silence me!"

The big one to begin with is social media, all varieties.

Many people realise it, but some don't; social media is often used only to promote success and happiness. Sadly, life isn't all success and happiness. Seeing people on social media you would think everything was brilliant all the time.

> *"Why are they always on holiday? Why do they only ever eat amazing food? Another promotion? They got another new car? That one's three times my annual salary!"*

People post like this because they seek acceptance. They want to show that in some way they are part of the crowd. It's safe being part of a herd. Only a few weak ones at the back get chomped, so just fit into the middle and it'll be okay.

En masse, however, this creates a false view for everyone! Regardless of whether you're having a great time or not, on those few occasions when you look and you are not, all you will see is people who are apparently happier than you are.

Sheep in the middle of the flock just follow where the dogs herd them. Only those on the edges can reasonably make decisions about their direction of travel.

> *"Ha. They're so happy. You're sat in your pyjamas with your cat alone!"*

I'm not going to tell you to abandon social media. It is part of our world now. I've tried to leave it and it's hard as it's engrained in everything. Leaving it is basically akin to cutting your ties to someone and burning down every bridge you had!

Still use it.

Still be a part of it.

Just take everything you see with a pinch of salt.

Take everything that comes up on your timeline, knowing that those people live the same sort of life as you.

I live alone. When I am at home by myself, I get anxious and agitated. Looking at social media makes this worse. I see so many people doing so many other things that I'm not doing. It stresses me out. I am slowly trying to just leave my phone and not look at it. It's easier said than done, but I think if I can master this then I might stand a chance of keeping him silent.

"You'll never silence me!"

Other ways to keep your inner critic muted are simply to not engage on the axes that you know upset you. This involves getting to know yourself and what really matters to you. If something is important to you and you know you could be hurt by discussing it with others, simply don't.

I for one refuse to talk politics with my parents. When politics comes up, I just say I don't want to talk about it. If they continue to talk about it and I feel uneasy; I leave the room. In this way I have protected my own beliefs and what matters to me, whilst respecting their decisions and wants.

"Can we talk about Brexit now?"

Just be honest.

Keep talking.

FACT

Remember that no one else out there can be a better you than you!

You already are the best you!

"No, you're not!"

The world may not be your oyster!

But you are the best person, and the only person, who can be you.

"What about Nathan Fillion?"

Every person is an individual. No two people are alike. No two people will experience anything the same way. No two people will respond identically.

You are more than the culmination of your experiences. You made every decision. You made every choice. You survived every failure. You are stronger, smarter, wiser and more knowledgeable than you were before. Regardless of what your inner critic might say, stand tall knowing that you got yourself here!

You might not like where here is!

But you know what?

You can move forward from here.

You have all your experiences to build upon. You have all the strength you've gained from going through everything you have done. Walk forward from here knowing that you can overcome whatever shit life throws at you.

Easier said than done.

I still don't believe in myself.

I still don't think I've achieved anything.

> *"Oh yeah, I'm not going anywhere. I'll be there to put you in your place when you least expect it. I'll make sure there's some part of you asking if you've made the right choice and if you're heading in the right direction. I'll be there on our death bed asking if our life meant anything."*

Remember though, that in the circumstances where your inner critic keeps shouting, can't be silenced, demands being listened to and just won't fucking shut up –

"..."

listen to it!

They are part of you. They're here to protect you and make sure you protect yourself. Sometimes not always in the best of ways, but that's purely logistical.

You should be proud of what you have achieved, regardless of whether society deems it to be an achievement. Who the fuck cares what society thinks? Be proud! You may be the woman at the top making the decisions or the guy in the factory fixing the machines; you have gotten yourself there and no one can judge you for what you've done as long as you're happy and you've not been a dick to anyone else along the way!

In the End

GONE

But being honest for a moment, who would really want to be me?

"No one would want to be you. You're awful."

Despite knowing that I wasn't a failure,

"You were."

my wife loved me but wanted to leave. My family loved me but had their own problems. My friends cared for me but had their own lives.

I felt I had nothing.

Even though from the outside it looked like I had everything.

I had nothing at all.

"Stupid sexy Flanders!"

When you have nothing in you, when you have nothing about you, it starts becoming all-encompassing. You become consumed. You start asking yourself questions you never thought you'd ask.

Do my friends like me? Or are they just using me?

Do my family like me? I know they love me, but do they like me?

Do I have a future in this world?

Would it be better if I wasn't around?

Would people be happier if I was gone?

You start looking at the world differently as well. The things that used to bring you joy in the slightest way stop doing so. You then attack yourself because you know you should feel something, but you don't. The pain rises and falls as waves ebb. The turmoil settles into numbness. The darkness consumes. You try to be happy but can't. You try to be sad but can't. You settle into the comfort that is the void of unfeeling. The void of everything!

This is depression.

This is my illness.

When people ask me what depression is and what it feels like I always give the same answer. Depression is this massive, heavy emptiness, like a black hole, that follows you round, making you feel heavier and heavier whilst consuming all your feelings. It doesn't just take the good, it takes the bad too. It leaves you numb and hollow.

The best depiction I have ever seen of depression is in a cartoon called *Big Mouth*.[17] Depression is shown to be this large purple cat that just sleeps on top of you and keeps you tired. It is the perfect representation for me. The only way I could see it being more perfect is if it was a black cat, but obviously that would be a pain to animate.

I have lived with depression most of my life. I was diagnosed during the last decade when I finally went and spoke to a doctor. I was scared about speaking to someone about how I was feeling. How can you even explain it?

---

[17] www.imdb.com/title/tt6524350 Accessed on 30/08/19

I'm just sad all the time. Not even sad. I just exist.

I was scared because of the perception around mental health depicted in television and movies. If I talked about how I was feeling, would I get sent to an asylum for the rest of my days? Would it be shock therapy and would I lose what little of my personality remained? I didn't know what to do, so I hid it all away, deep inside me.

Through experience, I can look back and see the themes and traits of mental illness throughout my life even before I was diagnosed. I can see it all the way back to my teenage years. I hid away in my room playing video games because there I was in a world where I was in control. I joined online communities. I built online communities. I sought acceptance from people I had never met because I found it easier that way. The emptiness I felt was briefly filled because I was distracted.

As I grew older, I would continue to do the same. I filled the emptiness I felt at university with alcohol and late nights. My first girlfriend broke up with me, sending me into a spiral of self-destructive behaviour which I barely survived. It cost me my upper second class degree. I hurt my friends. I hurt my peers. I hurt my family. I was lashing out because I didn't understand the pain I was feeling nor the emptiness that was consuming.

These cycles of self-destruction followed by recovery continued until I settled with my now ex-wife and even then, I still felt the waves coming and going.

The ebb and flow from the tides of the unfeeling void were relentless.

I was distracted caring for her at the beginning, supporting her through her chronic illness and helping her complete her PhD. It was only when her life settled that I really began to experience the pain and numbness again.

I was at a loss.

I thought it was gone.

"Did you miss me?"

And so, he returned.

I needed help.

DARK

I really needed help.

I needed real help.

At first, I was too ashamed, too scared and too stubborn to ask. I thought the people at work would find out and it would be an embarrassment I could never live down. I felt it would be the death knell of my career and that admitting this would effectively end my professional life.

I made excuses.

Eventually, after so much pain, I went to a doctor.

The conversation was awkward. 'Do you have any dark thoughts?'

"So many it would horrify you. How long do you have?"

Just ask if I'm suicidal please. Calling them dark thoughts to protect me isn't helpful. It just makes me feel worse about actually feeling suicidal. I am not a child. I need your help.

'Yes. I have dark thoughts.'

'I thought about ending my life last week.'

> *"Actual last week, but also historical last week. I love how meta my inputs can be!"*

After going through the motions, I was eventually prescribed some medication to help with the dark thoughts. This wasn't the first time I'd been on medication. When I was starting my career, I went onto citalopram[18] for a year or so to help with my anxieties around flying. I didn't know if it was doing anything, but it was comforting knowing that there was something there supposedly helping regardless. This time, however, I went onto sertraline.[19]

Most mental illness medication comes with the warning that it can take up to a month or so for your body to adapt to the new level of drugs in your body. They also come with warnings about how they work. In both instances, the drugs I was on were SSRIs (selected serotonin re-uptake inhibitors),[20] which basically prevent your body reabsorbing the hormone serotonin, effectively putting bands around your mood. You lose the lowest of lows but also lose the highest of highs. The painful bits go but you also lose some of the pleasure. It's a necessary evil.

---

[18] www.nhs.uk/medicines/citalopram Accessed on 05/09/19

[19] www.nhs.uk/medicines/sertraline Accessed on 05/09/19

[20] www.nhs.uk/conditions/ssri-antidepressants Accessed on 30/08/19

I started taking sertraline on a Thursday after seeing the doctor. I was going to London the next day to spend the weekend with my family. I didn't leave the hotel. I was nauseous beyond belief. I was having stomach spasms constantly. I hardly left the hotel room all weekend, opting to watch trash shows like *The 100*.[21] It was agony.

"The 100 wasn't that bad. Don't say it was agony!"

It certainly wasn't as bad as *Defying Gravity*.[22]

But, after about a week, my body slowly adapted. The pain was limited. The numbness faded. I was starting to feel again.

There was hope.

"The perception of hope is different from actual hope."

Things were on the up, but I still wasn't feeling right, I lacked confidence and I had incredibly low self-esteem. I was weak and I was worried about the perception of being on medication. I was unsure of myself and unsure of the decisions I was making.

Again, I needed help.

I am sceptical of most things. It comes with being professional. You're paid to manage risk and to anticipate it. When my ex-wife suggested I go speak to a counsellor to talk about my confidence and how I was feeling, I laughed.

---

[21] www.imdb.com/title/tt2661044 Accessed on 30/08/19

[22] www.imdb.com/title/tt1319690 Accessed on 05/09/2019

Eventually after weeks, maybe even months, of feeling insecure I accepted that I couldn't do this alone. My ex-wife was seeing a counsellor herself and it was helping her a lot. Little did I know at the time where it would lead.

"The L-word. Lesbian? Lesbians?"

I turned to the internet and found the first person in the counselling directory who didn't specialise in Cognitive Behavioural Therapy. This is the NHS default approach and I fucking hate it. If I felt I could change the way I responded to situations just by 'making myself' think differently, don't you think I'd have already tried it?! I could see this working in some circumstances, but it's just not something I was interested in.

I went into my first appointment with my counsellor nervous. Were they going to delve into my past? Were they going to pull apart my psyche? Was it all because I have daddy issues?

"You do have daddy issues! You aspire to be him and yet strive to be as different as you can. You're fucked up!"

I walked into the room. Sat on the chair. My heart was racing. 'How're you doing then, Andy?'

What? Is this a trick question? What does it mean? Am I being lured into a false sense of security?

Nope.

This is what it is.

This is therapy.

Or at least, this is my therapy.

Just talking to someone is therapy. It took me a long time to adjust to it and to figure it out. It took time to become confident enough to be open. I was embarrassed saying that I went to therapy every week.

This has all changed.

One Friday morning, my therapist said to me something along the lines of 'Walking through that door', gesturing towards the door to their room, 'is a sign of real strength'. Walking into a room and asking a stranger to help you is a sign that you want to fight for yourself.

I did want to fight for me.

> *"Did you though? Did you really? No one wants to fight for Andy."*

I think.

I now recommend therapy, counselling, whatever; just talk to someone about what's going on in your life and in your head. It doesn't need to be all psychology and deep philosophical debates about 'who you really are'. My best therapy sessions are the ones where we just talk. Recently these sessions have been about this book and how I am nervous of the results.

I hope I haven't let you down!

> *"You mean like you let down everyone else around you every day?"*

However, just as I was beginning to pull myself out of my hole and get myself back on track. My wife left me.

Everything shattered.

Everything was gone.

All that was left was the numb darkness of the void.

It was staring at me.

I couldn't stop staring back.

It ate through the walls and defences that I had built over the years. It consumed everything in its path. The sertraline did nothing to help. I was left empty and numb.

This time it was beyond what I had ever felt before.

I couldn't continue.

So, I did what any person of reasonably sound mind would do.

I decided I was going to kill myself.

> *"Classic bait and switch there. Love it."*

CIAO

Ending your life is not a quick decision. You don't come to this conclusion overnight. You spend hours, days, weeks and months thinking about it. Is it the right thing to do? Is it for the best? Is this how it all ends? You find things each time to keep yourself going. You find a reason to continue. It's often small and inconsequential. You just keep finding reasons.

This time I couldn't find anything. This time I was done. There was nothing left to fight for. It was all gone. All I had was misery and misery was all I brought to those around me. I had failed at everything I ever even tried to attempt and was left with nothing to show for it.

"You may feel he's being melodramatic with some of this language, but it's all true. This is what I was telling him. If you don't believe him then at least believe me. I'm the honest one of the two of us."

I started researching how to end my life.

I didn't want to go outside as I was so ashamed of what I was going through. I didn't want to see other people as I was too embarrassed. Oddly enough, I didn't want anyone to have to clean up any mess or see it happen. I didn't want to cause more pain to more people. I just wanted to go quietly and be forgotten. I wanted to fade into the unknown obscurity that I felt I deserved. In time no one would remember me. They'd be better off without me.

I eventually settled on hanging myself.

Relatively quick. Relatively painless. Relatively easy to do. What more could you want really?

My issue was where and with what. My house wasn't designed with hanging in mind; I'm not sure many are.

I quickly realised there was only one place in my house where it would work. It would rely on a bit of luck and some quick calculations to work out if I needed more than one belt to support my body weight. I didn't want a failed attempt because I was a fatty.

"Fucking weirdo. Just get it done with. It shouldn't be taking this long!"

It was settled.

Quick check of everything around my computer. I quickly glanced over Facebook to see if there was anything to keep me here. I checked online to see if anyone was asking me any questions. I checked my phone for any messages that needed a reply.

Nope.

No reason to stay then.

See you later.

"Well. No. You're killing yourself."

I walked into my bedroom, my marital bedroom from my once loving marital home. I went and found my belts, selecting the two finest leather belts, snapping them to make sure they were tight. I had a tear in my eye knowing that what I was about to do was going to hurt people. The pain would dull. Time heals all wounds. They would heal in time.

"What about your wounds?"

Sky and Roxy were fussing around me, but my mind was made up. I stood up from the bed slowly and began walking towards the stairs that led up to the top floor.

This was it.

I'd be free soon.

It would all be over soon.

BEER

The phone on my desk buzzed.

I paused.

Sadly, I can't remember the exact details of what happened here. You know, I was a little preoccupied with trying to kill myself and all that.

A message from my best friend.

Bit of background.

We are a terrible influence on each other. We organise stupid things like 'The Vodka Challenge'. All you can drink for the night is vodka, and mixers, we're not monsters. The last person standing wins.

Sounds smart, doesn't it?

We both outdrank the competition by quite some way and eventually called it a draw. We danced like no one was watching for the rest of the night as all our other friends gave up and went home.

Not us though. We weren't quitters!

"I can't even stop you when you two are together."

We couldn't stand a draw so a year or so later we had 'The Tequila Challenge'. No guessing the rules for this one. This time no friends were involved. It was a head-to-head. It was on! We cooked our dinner in tequila. We made tequila jelly. We had margaritas and shots all night.

Another draw.

We have never let each other down. Over almost fifteen years of friendship, whenever the call came in, from either one of us, we were there. We have each other's backs! We don't quit on each other!

Anyway, back to the point at hand: I was about to kill myself!

"Sometimes I wish you had used a point! Might have been faster!"

The message I read was something along the lines of, 'Are you still good to come out and play next week?', paraphrased as 'Let's go drinking'.

"Always."

Always.

She had been through a rough patch herself and had been struggling. Don't get me wrong, I win 'The Baggage Challenge' by a fucking mile; not much can trump a lesbian ex-wife.

"You're literally Ross Geller."

Despite everything going on in her life, as soon as I told her that my ex-wife and I were separating, she was on the train from London to Leeds to be there for me. I even remember the post she put on Facebook after we spoke that night.

She was still here. She survived her rough patch. She did it alone. She made it through. If she can do it, why can't I?

I can't lose a challenge to her.

I can't drop out of the race.

I am not a quitter.

I may have failed in business. I may have failed as a husband. I have failed as a cat parent. I may have failed as a son, a brother, a friend and even as a fucking person.

But I am not going to fail this time.

I'm not going to let her beat me at simply existing by default.

"The two greatest words in the English language!"

I dropped the belts to the ground. I looked at Sky and Roxy who were with me, wondering what the hell I was doing.

I replied.

'ofc'

And just like that, life finds a way.

When I felt I was worth nothing, when I felt I had nothing, when I felt there was no reason to be, no reason to live – a simple message from a friend, my best friend, reminding me that I was wanted in this world changed everything for me.

It is something I'll never forget.

It is a debt I can never repay.

People often ask me how to help someone suffering or struggling with their mental health. It could be a colleague, friend or family member.

The honest answer is that you can't help someone until they want helping.

You can't help them until they are ready for help. All you can do is make sure they know someone is there, no matter what.

Do not give up on them.

Never give up on them.

Make them know they have a friend. Make them know they have a family member. Make them know they have someone!

When they are ready, they will turn to the people who have never stopped being there for them. When they are ready, you will be able to help them. It can feel like a thankless task that they may never acknowledge, but you are making a difference, even if you can't see it or feel it.

Leave no one behind.

Ever.

The Weight of Shame

HOLD

I was alive.

I wasn't expecting it.

The fog lifted. It was a sudden shock. I didn't really know what to think or what to do. There was a rush of adrenaline. I knew I had to do something, but I didn't know what. I tried to calm myself. I slowed my breathing.

> *"You failed at everything and then failed at ending your life. You're the worst."*

As I slowed down, I realised that I never wanted to feel like that again.

"You've failed at that too!"

I started thinking. I'm one in almost eight billion; there must be more people out there like me, so I started looking into the statistics.

I wanted to do something to help those out there who might be struggling like I was. I wanted to give others the benefit of my rather shit experiences so that maybe, just maybe, they could avoid my innumerable mistakes. I wanted to let people know that they were not alone, no matter what their circumstances.

"You were still alone though. Was this yet another distraction?"

I repositioned what I was doing in my spare time. I put an emphasis on raising money for mental health charities. I encouraged the various gaming communities I was part of to promote positive mental health. I wanted people to feel comfortable being who they are.

Finally.

After much deliberation.

After much pain.

I finally told my parents.

I remember sitting on a sofa in my dad's study with the sun on our faces. I was in tears. I was crying and I couldn't stop. I tried to explain that I didn't want to keep going, but that I did now and that I was okay. He didn't understand. I told him that I had called the Samaritans.

He still didn't really understand. I told him I had tried to kill myself, but I stopped. That's when he understood. He hugged me. He held me. He was in tears too. He hadn't appreciated what I was experiencing.

In this moment, I realised that not only did I not want people to feel how I felt; I also wanted to educate those who didn't understand these feelings in the first place.

This was the moment where all this nonsense started.

I still can't believe how far I've come from that point.

GAIN

The journey from then to this book is relatively quick.

Less than eighteen months, give or take!

It all starts somewhere, and for me it started with World of Warcraft.

> *"I didn't say you could talk about this! It's been almost fifteen years of our life!"*

The new World of Warcraft expansion was coming out. There was hype.

> *"It wasn't hype worthy!"*

I wanted to do something special for it, so I decided I would do a twenty-four-hour live charity stream. For those unsure, I was basically committing to playing a computer game for twenty-four hours consecutively whilst people could watch me on the internet and any donations raised during that time would be given to charity.

"Please like and subscribe. Click that little bell icon. It all really helps."

I knew I would get support.

But I wanted this to be big.

I wanted to do more.

An idea was born.

What if I told my professional network about it? They're typically wealthy and will often support a good cause. I've never done it before. I am not one of those people who does charity runs or stuff like that. What can I do to raise the awareness of this with them? How about I write an article and post it on LinkedIn? They'll probably read it if I write it well enough. They'll probably give a little bit, but it'll slowly add up. I'll get a few 'aww' and 'good on you' posts. It'll be good and it'll make a difference.

Combine this with my friends and family and maybe I'll raise one hundred pounds or so.

I knew that I was going to speak honestly. I was going to be as blunt as possible and get this heard. Can't worry about the future now, I almost didn't have one! I sat down at eight in the morning one Saturday and started writing. By eleven I was finished. I published the article, without review, and then went about my day as usual.

"You still haven't learned how to review your work. It's embarrassing!"

'Read this or don't. The choice is yours.' It started. 'Breaking the Stigma - by Andy Salkeld.' I carried on and simply said, 'My name is Andy Salkeld. I live with depression. I have done so for many years. In 2017, I almost took my own life.' It went on, discussing the statistics, talking about the stream and raising money for charity.

It was described as searingly honest.

This was my acceptance. This was me accepting myself. This was me coming to terms with who I am. This was me standing up and being me.

At this point in my life I had kept everything inside. I bottled up all those feelings, all that shame and all that regret. I let it fester. This was me accepting all of that and then casting it aside.

I was at peace with myself.

There was still a roil in the sea of feelings and emotions below me, but for the first time in a long time, I had risen above it. It was calm.

"Not for long."

I thought peace would come from ending my life.

Instead peace came from embracing my life and accepting myself.

Funny when you think about how similar, yet how different, those are. I had broken my own bonds and was now free. I couldn't give a shit what people thought anymore. If they have a problem with me, that's on them. I am going to be myself and I am going to be happy in doing so.

Thousands of views. Hundreds of likes and shares. 'Breaking the Stigma' broke my expectations!

Then the phone rang.

I was asked if I would like to speak about my experiences on World Mental Health Day.

I love public speaking.

I thrive on an audience.

I didn't need to think about the answer.

I immediately said yes.

I immediately started drafting some slides.

"You're such a fucking geek."

WILL

I had fire again.

I had passion.

Yes, my emotions and feelings were still dulled by the drugs in my system, but I cared about something. I was making a difference. It wasn't big. It wasn't special. It was just one talk. I would do it at the cost of nothing, in front of complete strangers, tell it how it is, and hopefully, some of them would take something away and maybe, just maybe, they would feel slightly more at ease talking themselves. Maybe a slightly more mentally healthy culture would be born as a result. But if not, I've done what I can and will find more ways to help others.

This was where all this began.

Now I've written a fucking book on it all.

A fucking book.

Me.

You're reading it!

Everything in my life changed and for the better.

Why?

I stopped being ashamed of who I was or who I am.

All the bullying. All those critics. The countless failures. My lost time, energy and spoons! I stopped being ashamed of it.

This is who I am.

I'm a decent-ish, alright-ish guy.

I'm just another guy.

I don't need to stand out. I don't need to be the best. I can just be.

I now fight for something I believe in. I have passion about something. I still don't value myself or my failures, but I value this and what I do; in turn it gives me value. We will come onto purpose in the next chapter but know that this is where I found my purpose, even if I didn't realise it till much later.

Having something you believe in and something to strive for makes us human. We as a species push ourselves forward continuously. We are not a race to stand still.

Whilst the race may not stand still, you can!

And that's the whole point! You don't need to worry about time passing by. You don't need to worry about missing out on something.

What will happen, will just happen.

If you are lost or struggling, try to find something, anything. It doesn't need to be something grandiose like 'Breaking the Stigma' was for me. It just needs to be something you care about.

People are the reason I fight! People and cats.

"Cats. Cats. Cats!"

As soon as my life settled – after the separation, after the house sale, after a move into a new flat – I adopted a kitten called Pika. I fight for her.

I fight for all my friends. I especially fight for my best friend, the one who kept me here. I want to be able to go to the pub with her when we're old and grey, look back on our youth and think: 'What the fuck? We were such kids! We were so stupid!', as we compete in the inevitable 'Yorkshire Tea Challenge'.

Be true to yourself. Be true to those around you. Embrace who you are and accept yourself and all your flaws and failings. Enjoy yourself and what you enjoy. Care for yourself and what you care about.

Be yourself.

No one else can be you.

EIGHT

FUCK IT AND GO FIND YOUR IKIGAI

That Moment

LEWD

Now we're going to flip everything on its head. This chapter is the culmination of everything we've learned so far and puts it all into an easy-to-understand and simple-ish diagram. But first, some stories!

When I started my career in the Big Four it was a whirlwind of training and events across the country. There were sessions on dressing to impress and what the colour of your shirt meant.

"Sometimes. Always. Never."

There were sessions on accounting, audit and tax too!

There was one course, however, that I will never forget. It fundamentally changed the way I approach work and life. It was a bullshit course like no other.

It was a course about soft skills.

For those uncertain, soft skills involve things like handshakes, eye contact and mannerisms. Later in my career I would build upon these teachings by doing a course on negotiation, which basically just says, 'Make sure not to give anything away through your soft skills.'

It was the afternoon session. We'd spent the morning walking round trying to shake hands with people who only wanted to look at our shoes. Anything would be interesting at this point!

"Professional training at its finest."

There was the usual preamble: some 'ice breaker' to try and get people talking and slightly more energetic after a sedentary lunch.

We were sat down and the tutor started speaking: 'Blah blah blah…, if you can find something you enjoy doing, then you should do it for a job.'

"Anything other than accounting then?"

He continued: 'Blah blah…, needs to be something you really love. Not just something you like. It needs to be something you would be willing to do ten hours a day, every day of every week of every month of every year for the rest of your life. Never tiring. Never getting bored. Always wanting to do it again and again. If you can find that one thing, then you will never feel like you are working, and you will be your happiest self.'

Silence.

'But sir.'

Someone broke the silence.

'We can't all be porn stars.'

Laughter.

The room erupted.

It was a good joke delivered with perfect timing. Everyone was in tears. The meaning of those deep and important words spoken to us faded into laughter and further jokes about who in the room would be the best and worst porn star.

We were young.

These words faded into the back of my memory. I would tell the story about the idea of being a porn star over again, but the real meaning of the words was forgotten until much later.

CASE

Skip forward about a decade.

I had sold my house and started the formal divorce process. Much of the pain I have talked about is now behind me, or at least, I don't feel it as much at this point. I am now in the process of finalising my investment in a tech start-up. Life is beginning to return.

I was invited to an event on a Friday night.

"Nope. Hate networking events."

I went along mostly out of boredom. I barely had a social life, I had no other plans and thought I should probably try to be social.

The talk began. It was standard and what I expected. The speaker was talking about the ten things every person can do to add value that require zero talent and cost nothing.[23] It includes things like 'being on time' and 'being prepared'. You know, the usual.

"Pleasantries."

But the speaker said there was an unwritten rule. One that supersedes all the others. Way more fundamental. Way more important.

---

[23] mollyfletcher.com/zero-talent Accessed on 30/08/19

'Don't be a dick.'

"Don't be a dick?"

'Don't be a dick' is a mantra I live by and one we will discuss in more detail later.

I sat up and started listening.

The speaker, who I am not ashamed to admit I was slowly developing a bit of a man crush on, started discussing the concept of the ikigai.[24]

Your ikigai, and it is something entirely personal, is a Japanese concept about purpose and fulfilment.

A Venn diagram appeared on screen and I was in heaven.

Your ikigai is the intersection of four parts of you and the world around you. If you can find something that satisfies all conditions, then you will have found your purpose in life and will experience fulfilment.

Suddenly my memory was flooded with laughter about the porn joke during my first weeks in practice. Fundamentally it was the same concept, but now there was context.

The speaker went on to discuss his mental health and wellbeing and how he had chosen to forgo over one million pounds' worth of future earnings to find a career

---

[24] 'The Japanese Concept "Ikigai" is a Formula for Happiness and Meaning'. *Better Humans*. https://medium.com/better-humans/the-japanese-concept-ikigai-is-a-formula-for-happiness-and-meaning-8e497e5afa99 Accessed 12/12/19

path that would not only earn the same if not more but would also bring him significantly more happiness.

"It's alright for some, isn't it?"

I was in awe.

It was definitely a crush.

So, what were the four areas of the Venn diagram that we need to consider?

What are you good at?

We've talked about this before. This is the concept of becoming an expert and applying your skills and abilities with confidence.

What do you enjoy?

Again, we've covered this. Finding enjoyment in your work is incredibly important to maintaining your mental health and wellbeing as work takes up almost a third of your life.

What can you be paid for?

We haven't covered this in detail, but it makes sense. If you cannot be paid for it, it is more of a hobby or pastime than a job.

What does the world need?

Here's the doozy. Here's the challenging bit. Is whatever you are good at and enjoy doing, that some people, somewhere, are willing to pay for, needed? Yes, people may be willing to pay for it. People will pay for a lot of things. But is it needed? Specifically, is your version of it needed?

Is it really needed?

The short answer is probably.

If someone is willing to pay for something, then at least one person in the world needs it.

"Like 'used gamer-girl bathwater'? Seriously, go look up Belle Delphiny!"[25]

Be cautious though.

It may not actually be the product or service you think you are providing that the world needs. It could be something closely aligned, but not that specific kernel you believe it to be.

Understanding what that kernel of need is will help you unlock your ikigai and find fulfilment and purpose.

Just remember though.

We can't all be porn stars.

"We can in here! Winky face!"

Eww.

POLL

Before we talk about my ikigai, how I found it and what to consider in searching for yours, I just want to mention where being an accountant fits for me into the four quadrants.

Does the world need it?

---

[25] www.instagram.com/belle.delphiny Accessed on 30/08/19

Yes. Death and taxes. Accountants are needed and you'll never be without a job with an accounting qualification. Same with lawyers. We're parasites. Parasites always have a feeding ground. We survive on both life and death.

Can you get paid for it?

Yes. Accountants have some of the most stable income streams of any profession. Their work is regulated and a necessity in our economy. This will continue until capitalism fails us.

"Please."

Accountants will always be highly sought after and highly paid. Again, same with lawyers. We're all necessary evils in this world.

Are you good at it?

Probably. I don't know. I'm not confident about it. My own imposter syndrome and insecurities make me question whether I'm good at anything. Sure, I have a qualification, but that doesn't mean I'm good at it. Look at all the bad drivers on the roads!

Do I enjoy it?

I didn't enjoy the numbers. I didn't enjoy the modelling. I enjoyed some of the problem solving. I enjoyed designing presentations. What I enjoyed the most though was face-to-face communication. I enjoyed talking. I enjoyed communication. Hardly a large part of the job though.

Fairly easy to see from this that being an accountant wasn't my ikigai!

I might make a half decent porn star come to think of it.

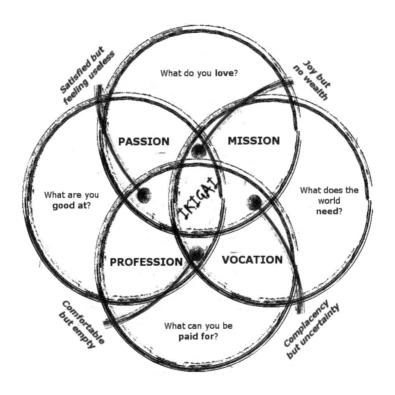

We're Half-Way There

GOAL

What do you care about?

It doesn't matter if it's something you're good at or something you get paid for, just whether you enjoy it and the world needs it. I always talk about this as the 'campaigning' part of the ikigai.

> *"Like a Dungeons & Dragons campaign?"*

If you would go to a rally, convention, parade, fundraiser or anything of the like, out of choice, then this is one of your missions in life.

Some easy examples are things like Pride and climate change.

> *"Or becoming a Pokémon Master, like no one ever was?"*

No.

These don't always have to be macro things. You can also have micro drives.

> *"Mr Bond."*

For a lot of people, this is family.

We want to raise another generation of 'us' to keep our families going. This drive is behind why people will say things like 'I'll do anything for my kids.' They are driven to protect their family.

Knowing what drives you and pushes, or pulls, you forward is important in any decision you make regardless of your career or life.

It doesn't need to be grandiose.

You just need to care about it!

FIRE

You enjoy it and you are good at it. It doesn't matter if you're paid or if the world needs it; you're doing it just because of the delight it brings you.

These are often hobbies, pastimes and other recreational activities. You don't do them for the greater good and you don't get paid for them.

You do them for fun.

But what if you could get paid for them?

This would be the dream, wouldn't it?

I'm sure we've all said it to ourselves at one time or another: 'I wish I could do this for my job.' Playing golf, playing football, shopping; whatever it is, someone somewhere has daydreamed about turning that hobby into their job.

"Who daydreams about being an accountant?

The important part of your passion when considering your ikigai is looking deeper than just the surface.

My best example of this is with my enjoyment of video games. Why do I like them? What do they give me that I can't find elsewhere?

Escapism? Not really, I can find that elsewhere.

Narrative? Again, no, there are many narratives out there.

Strategy! I like the complexity of micro and macro management.

Competition! I love competing with other players.

Community! I love being part of a bigger community.

Looking below the surface reveals that it isn't the video games I like; it is the human aspect that comes with them.

I am passionate about playing games with and against other people.

For me, it's always been about the people!

WORK

This is where a lot of people end up.

They get paid to do something that the world needs.

It's sad.

It's soulless.

It's true.

In this quarter there is little happiness and enjoyment from the work you're doing and you're not even necessarily any good at it.

This is about survival.

It isn't impossible to escape from here. What you're missing is enjoyment and expertise.

Expertise can easily come with practice. Keep doing the job, learn more about it, expand your knowledge, question why!

Enjoyment is harder to find. We all enjoy different things and would spend our time differently if we had the choice. Finding enjoyment in your work is important and will keep you going when the work is mundane.

This again comes back to understanding yourself and what matters to you.

I enjoy learning, so I always want to be learning. If I feel I don't know or don't understand something, then I will try to teach myself. It's a challenge and it keeps me interested, even whilst bored. If I ever reach a stage in a job where I am bored or there is nothing to challenge me, or nothing more to learn, I leave.

Someone recently called me Nanny McPhee. I had no idea what it meant until they explained it further.

> *"When you need me, but do not want me, then I will stay. When you want me, but do not need me, then I have to go."*

GIFT

You've got wits. You've got looks. You've got passion.

> *"Don't start singing."*

You're good at it and you can get paid for it.

This is one of the best building blocks from which to find your ikigai. You will be able to achieve great satisfaction from doing something you are good at and getting paid for it.

The problem though is you may not enjoy it and it might not be necessary, leaving you in an ambivalent state of fear, never knowing if you're valued for your abilities and never really enjoying it due to the uncertainty.

Your life here is often about process.

Process is a necessary evil in large corporations and practices. Process brings consistency in delivery. With good processes in place it's easy to identify where errors and mistakes occur.

I, however, am not a fan of process.

"How the hell are you an accountant again?"

When I know what needs to be done, I just want to get it done. When I'm bound by the leash of red tape and strangled in the chains of hierarchy, it suffocates me.

Finding enjoyment in your skills or turning your skills towards something you can enjoy will help move you towards your dreams.

It isn't always easy to do this, and it can be challenging to find the opportunities that allow it; but when you achieve it, you will be one step closer to your ikigai.

Three Quarter Pounder

EASE

You are good at something; you enjoy it and are even getting paid for it; but the world doesn't really need it.

This is not a common place to think of being until you realise that many of these sorts of jobs no longer exist.

These jobs have now typically been automated where they can be so that they are no longer draining on resources.

"Human Resources."

Why pay for something if it's not really needed after all?

Nowadays, the jobs that result in this stage of the ikigai are often bureaucratic in nature, focused on maintaining order and regulation in line with whatever organisation or structure they are in.

I felt I was here when I worked in assurance. I was good at it; I could tick and bash like the best of them. I enjoyed its simplicity. I was getting paid well for it. But as many auditors will attest, you do not feel respected by the client. You're a statutory requirement. You're there to fulfil a legal obligation. You add no value to the operations of the business. You command no respect. You just get in the way.

It's miserable.

If you find yourself in a position like this, take some time to consider your options. My honest recommendation if you feel unnecessary is to move on. It is one of the worst feelings I have ever felt; and one that even now reminds me of how I felt during my darkest depression.

REST

This is a typical resting place for many.

It is where many people stay in their careers.

They are just one step away from fulfilment but can't, or won't, escape their comfort zone and take that final risky step to achieve the ikigai.

You can't really blame them!

You are good at something; the world needs it and you are getting paid for it. Sadly though, you don't necessarily enjoy it. This is often where many people end up in their mid-life. They've trained for a long time and have pushed themselves forward to become experts.

However, they aren't happy with the field they've become an expert in. Or there is just something that is preventing them from being happy in it.

This is where I was.

As much as I have confidence issues and struggle with imposter syndrome about whether I should be an accountant, I am good at risk management and finance. I can build complex financial models. I learned how to program and built systems from scratch. I understand the inner workings of financial and operational systems.

But I wasn't happy.

I needed to bring enjoyment into my work somehow.

I just didn't know how!

SMUG

This is where imposter syndrome fits in.

You're getting paid for something that is needed and it's providing you with happiness and enjoyment. But you don't know if you're any good at it.

This leaves you with a constant fear of being 'found out'.

"At some point the readers will realise you are just talking nonsense."

Many people will end up in this category regardless of whether they are very good at it or not. The belief that you are not qualified for your role is just as bad as not being qualified for your role.

It is a hard place to escape.

You know this.

I know this.

We've talked about this in previous chapters.

The only way you can move on from this point is to start to believe in yourself.

"Neo."

Obviously, if you are truly incompetent at your job, you should probably just do the appropriate qualifications and training to build your competence and confidence.

GLEE

This is one of the hardest parts of the ikigai to escape.

It is where many people end up with their hobbies and interests but ultimately become unwilling to take the necessary risks to achieve the ikigai.

You have a skill that you are good at, you love doing it and the world wants it.

Your problem is purely one of monetising.

If anyone has ever said to you 'You should do this for a job' or 'Have you thought of selling this?' then this is where you have landed.

This isn't to say you can't try to monetise it. In fact, you should try to monetise it! If you can, you will have found your ikigai. What stops people here is a lack of knowledge about how to monetise, or a fear of failure with monetising.

Often confidence plays a huge issue here.

There is risk in trying to turn something you love into something that provides for you and your family.

You are essentially opening up yourself and asking the world to 'value' you. This is brave. What if people don't want to pay for this? What if people only want to pay a low value for this?

"Failure."

Nope.

You just have a hobby that you are incredibly good at and the world and people enjoy, but just aren't willing to pay for, or are unwilling to pay the price you want.

Nothing has changed, but at least you tried!

You can continue enjoying it or make appropriate changes to enable a sale but there is nothing to stop you doing this as a hobby for pure enjoyment.

As an aside, my talks and even this book are very much me trying to move out of this stage of the ikigai. It's a risk I've taken, exposing me, my life and my deepest self to the world, saying, 'I want this to be what I do from now on. I want to give myself to help others. Please help me in this cause.'

The Full Package

HANG

I have heard this time and time again and it always resonates with me.

Accountants, like lawyers, are money rich and time poor.

I'm sure this applies to most roles in other professional services as well as to most jobs even outside of the professional sector. People who work hard exchange their personal time for additional money. This concept was explained to me during my first year of practice and has stuck with me ever since.

This is also the argument whenever people talk about moving to a four-day working week. Would you be willing to take a twenty percent cut on your salary to work only four days?

> *"I mean, of course, but would we actually be doing twenty percent less work as well? Otherwise it's just doing more in less time which isn't worth it."*

It's important to know where you want to end up on this seesaw. Would you rather be someone who has more spare time available for self-actualisation at the opportunity cost of your earnings and ability to spend disposable income in your spare time? Or would you rather have more disposable income so that you could have a much more extravagant experience in your spare time but have less time in which to spend it?

On the following diagram you will see that the time sacrificed to achieve more money comes with significant diminishing returns as you need to build the base out before you can add height. This is apt because it is a true representation of reality, as only by sacrificing more and more of those 'non-working' hours that we talked about in Chapter Two can we achieve the greatest riches and rewards. It's also apt because it is how torque[26] and moments work in real life!

"Science! Bitch!"

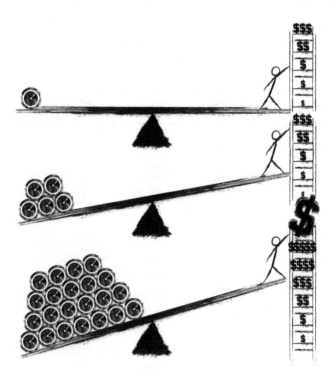

[26] Serway, R. A. and Jewett, Jr. J. W. (2003). *Physics for Scientists and Engineers,* sixth edition. Pacific Grove, CA: Brooks Cole

One thing I only realised after drawing this was that the 'super wealthy mega money' is crushing the bottom rungs of the ladder above it. It wasn't intentional at all, but it's an apt representation of capitalism and the world we live in today so I just wanted to highlight it.

I personally am not one for expensive and fancy things. I do not wear branded clothing. I don't have expensive hobbies. My only extravagances in life are travelling to see my friends and my cat, Pika. I don't take expensive holidays and am mostly happy to stay in the UK to reduce air travel. I don't buy stuff for the sake of buying it and I try to find enjoyment in creation and in spending time with people, rather than in things and objects. I prefer having experiences and building memories than owning stuff!

As such, I'm much happier having more time.

Yes, I come from a wealthy family, I won't deny that. Yes, I have done well for myself in my career, I won't deny that either. But I would be just as happy with very little, doing things much cheaper, if it afforded me the time to enjoy life.

"No amount of money ever bought a second of time."

TIME

When considering where you sit on the seesaw, and how this relates to your ikigai, remember what we considered back in Chapter Two.

Time is finite.

Money is not.

You will live your days and then you will die. That will be the case regardless of how much money you ever have in your possession. Money can potentially be infinite.

Time is therefore a relatively scarce resource and hence should command a higher price under the fundamental principles of supply and demand.[27] You can earn any amount of money and its value will fluctuate within reason in the economic climate at the time. Time is different. Time being finite means that the less time you have remaining the more valuable it becomes. The value you place on time will naturally increase as you age.

This is why retirement is a goal for many people. You get all of your time and can spend it how you wish!

So why don't we value time as much beforehand? Is there a point where money is more valuable?

Consider the current millennial generation; they are more driven by experiences and by the accumulation of 'life' than by money. They will work hard, but prioritise time off, holidays, flexible working arrangements, the ability to work abroad, the ability to continue to study, the ability to work with charities and more. They want their time on our little blue planet to mean something and seek ways to achieve that.

Ultimately how much you value time and money is up to you.

---

[27] https://quickonomics.com/the-law-of-supply-and-demand/ Accessed 12/12/19

For me, my time and my wellbeing far outweigh any amount of money.

HELP

So, after thinking about all these things and considering where I wanted to sit on the time-money seesaw, where did I end up?

For me life is about helping others.

Which is a far cry from Past Andy who could only think about helping himself.

"So selfish."

I knew I always loved social interaction. I knew I found great pleasure in teaching and helping people to learn and grow. I also love being the centre of attention and standing out; but I like doing this as me, not as something else, something false.

What I have realised is that I was getting parts of this from all my previous jobs, roles and hobbies but was never getting to do it as myself in a way I wanted.

This book and hopefully all the books that follow,

"I didn't agree to write this book; don't you dare go committing to more books now!"

my talks and hopefully all the talks that follow will become my reason for being.

These are my ikigai.

This is what I am passionate about and what I see as my purpose.

By buying this book you have helped me to be one step closer to achieving my dream and in turn I truly hope this book helps you get at least one step closer to achieving yours.

I want to help others grow through sharing my experiences and failures. I want to guide people through the storm that is life and help them become the heroes of their own story.

NINE

LEARNING TO LOVE LEMONS BECAUSE YOU'RE SICK OF LEMONADE

Disney Lied to Us!

CRAP

Let's get one thing straight before I go into a monologue of misery: I'm not a pessimist. I'm quite the optimist. I trust people and believe in what they say, despite being trained to think otherwise. I believe in upside and get excited at opportunities. I'm not blind to the risks, I just believe that people will work hard if supported and given the opportunity.

I'm also a realist.

Empirical evidence and facts outweigh belief.

Maybe what I say will be because of that tainted image.

"Almost certainly. You are bitter and twisted after all."

Maybe there's truth in it.

Regardless, this is my fundamental belief:

Don't be a dick and be happy.

If you can do these two things, you're golden. All the dicks in the world are typically seen that way because of their dickishness towards others. Don't be a dick. Simple.

This chapter is about stepping back from yourself and finding your place in the bigger tapestry of life. There is a lot you cannot control and worrying about those things will never lead to anything worthwhile. These are my opinions; don't feel you have to agree with me!

It's my book afterall. I can say what I like.

"Waits for copy editor to take this bit out."

LEAF

Despite what we are led to believe, we are not all equal.

I've been saying this throughout the book. You are beautifully unique. The extension to everyone not being equal shouldn't be too much of a stretch!

Nature and nurture have a massive influence on who you are and what you can achieve. It would be great to believe that anyone can achieve anything their heart desired, but it's simply not the case.

Our parents lied to us!

Our schools lied to us!

Disney lied to us!

You have no control over your genetics. If you're born a mermaid, there is no sea witch to help you walk under the sun. That prince won't notice you as you sing out on Siren's Rock. Your genetics have bound you under the sea and you're not part of his world.

Sucks.

Likewise, there are so many other things that your genetics control.

> *"You're fat. You have bad skin. You can't grow facial hair. You have depression. You wear glasses. You snore. You have asthma. You have that annoying hairy mole on your arm. I can keep doing this all day!"*

This can work in your favour. Exceptional individuals do appear! We wouldn't have people like Einstein[28] or Hawking[29] without such uncontrolled genetics.

> *"We've always had a bit of a man crush on Hawking if we're honest."*

Sometimes it might not. You might have allergies. You might have intolerances. You might even have issues producing serotonin, dopamine, oxytocin and the other 'happy hormones' which can be a physical cause of depression, anxiety and more.

> *"You're doing that weirdly specific thing again."*

Just as we spoke in earlier chapters about focusing your time and effort on things in work you can control, focus on the parts of your life and body you can control.

As a human race, we've built a surprisingly large industry about trying to improve our genetics or at least hide them: dentists, hair dyes, razor blades, contact lenses, hair straighteners, makeup and more. These all exist to adjust what our genetics define.

I for one have accepted that I will never be skinny.

> *"Fatty."*

I still try to maintain my health through exercise and healthy eating. I don't stress about what the scales say because I don't own any! I worry more about whether I

---

[28] www.biography.com/scientist/albert-einstein Accessed on 06/09/19

[29] www.hawking.org.uk Accessed on 06/09/19

feel healthy, whether I'm sleeping well and whether I feel confident in my body.

"You don't feel that healthy, you never sleep well and you don't have any confidence in your own skin. What the hell are you on about?"

I have also accepted my depression. I have accepted that it's part of me and that I need the help of the anti-depressants to lead a life I am happy with.

"Okay with."

There's no point worrying about the parts of your nature you can't change. It's easy to get sucked into trying to correct nature rather than embrace it!

Nature is nature.

And just like life.

Nature finds a way.

LUCK

Now I'm not going to hide away from it; I am incredibly lucky to have my family.

They are wealthy in a way I will never really understand. It's all self-made. Nothing came through inheritance. They started on council estates in Middlesbrough. My parents are the children of a miner, a dinner lady, a milk man and a milk lady. They have achieved what is almost impossible nowadays in terms of social mobility.

They have stood by me and supported me throughout all my failures and misgivings.

Even though I have worried about whether they like me as a person and whether I'm slowly but surely being cut off and abandoned, I know they love me, and I know they'll support me in the future if my world collapses again.

"I give it ten years or so."

When people say 'It's not what you know, it's who you know' never forget that you know your family and that they will want to do more for you than anyone else. I personally find it very hard to ask for help from my family. I believe that if I am to fail, I want it to be my own failure. Likewise, if I succeed,

"Ha!"

I want it to be my own success. I know I can turn to them, but I always try to avoid it as I want to be responsible for myself. I've started turning to them more over the years. It hurts my pride, but it helps my wellbeing.

It is a necessary sacrifice.

They also say, 'You can't choose your family.' Your family are there for you whether you like it or not.

I struggle with loneliness on a day-to-day basis, but I always remind myself that my family are there. When I'm feeling bad, I contact my family as I know regardless of the situation, they'll be there for me.

I am glad I overcame my issues with seeking help from my family. I may not like it, but I am in a better place now because of it!

Even if you're a diamond in the rough and obsessed with the Princess of a wealthy Sultan, remember who you really are. We don't get genies to grant us wishes and protect us from harm; sometimes we just need to embrace our inner scruff to let our true personality shine through.

Never be afraid to aim high and strive to achieve your dreams – you could end up in a whole new world. If you don't make it, you've still got yourself, your family and your pet monkey to keep you going.

> *"This is a weird mashup between Aladdin and Ross Geller, isn't it?"*

Why did you have to bring up the Ross Geller thing again?

ROCK

Life is unfair.

Life is inherently unfair.

If me telling you about how you're stuck with your genetics, how you can't change your family and how you're probably destined for a lifetime of mediocrity isn't enough, it's time to settle in for the bombshell.

You are not owed anything.

The universe owes you nothing.

You must struggle through life.

Fight for every shred of happiness.

Then you die.

You can work hard. You can be your best self. You can help everyone you ever meet. You can be completely selfless.

You can still get completely shat on. You may still never find love. You may also just get hit by a bus!

> *"Life's a bitch and then you die."*

Regardless of your race, your beliefs or the colour of your skin, whether you're a drunken dope addict or a glue sniffer, most people like to believe that there is something that means that their hardships will reward them in the end.

I'm sorry to say that this isn't the case.

You can work eleven hours a day in a mediocre job on a mediocre salary and never experience love, never find happiness and then die alone with no one ever visiting you in hospital and no one ever remembering your meaningless existence. The inevitable heat death of the universe follows slowly, and everything ultimately succumbs to entropy and nothingness.

> *"Stop it. This is my job."*

It is said it's better to have loved and lost than never to have loved at all. You at least have some fleeting memory of happiness to hold onto as your life leaves your body.

Remember though.

Disney lied to us.

Life is unfair.

There are no checks and counter-measures to ensure balance in happiness and sadness. In the very unfairness that we acknowledge we can find comfort.

Newton's Third Law states that every action has an equal and opposite reaction.

To shortcut trying to explain a complex point:

"Finally."

Your past has happened and whilst you can learn from it, don't let it dictate your present. Your future isn't predetermined by your past, only by your present.

Taking control of your present is more important than anything else.

Focus on finding your happiness now.

Focus on living your life now.

Life can be shit. Life can be really shit. The shit may never stop flowing. But you don't know that. You don't know that the shit will never stop flowing. Equally, you don't know that the shit won't stop flowing tomorrow.

From someone who almost stopped having tomorrows, realise that it might just be worth hanging in there for just one more day to see if the shit does stop flowing. If it stops, great. If it doesn't, well, try again the next day. You just don't know!

It's why I believe in just loving lemons.

Because life will hand you them.

Life will hand you them, time and again.

You might have so many lemons that it just becomes impossible to make lemonade.

> *"Or even combustible lemons that burn houses down!"*

So, don't.

Don't even try.

Embrace it.

Find comfort knowing that this may be how it is now, but not necessarily how it will be tomorrow.

Life Is Shit but You Don't Have to Be

LIME

We've talked plenty about how you as an individual can make appropriate changes in your life and your decisions so you can improve your happiness and feeling of self-worth.

The hope is that if enough people start being more content in themselves, talking about their emotions and becoming happier overall, a better working environment, maybe even a better world, can be created as a result.

Until that point though, it's going to be an uphill struggle. The world is in pretty bad shape. Politics is a mess. There is distrust and loss of hope in the leadership of our countries. People are beginning to lose interest. Generations are divided and battle lines are slowly being drawn. The young versus the old. The former fighting for their very futures as the planet around them slowly dies; the latter striving to keep hold of wealth and power accumulated during their lives.

The world is struggling with an inevitable resource crisis where life may no longer be sustainable. Entire industries built around precious commodities may soon crumble as wars are waged over our finite resources. It's easy to see why certain people, companies and countries are looking at extreme options so as to overcome these issues.

The dystopian futures portrayed in popular science fiction feel ever more likely to become a reality with each passing day.

I have debated with people for hours on the exploration of other planets. Whilst previously I dreamed of seeing the stars, the exploration of space to overcome a man-made crisis feels like an ultimate failure. We have a planet that is more than capable of sustaining us as a species alongside all the different flora and fauna. We have consumed our way out of existence.

We don't deserve to find a habitable or terraformable planet.

"Agent Smith was right to call the human race a disease and a cancer!"

There is now a chance that our planet, our solitary planet, the only planet we know capable of sustaining any form of life, will be completely uninhabitable to human life within the next fifty years.[30]

Fuck.

Don't worry, you get a choice of how you go out!

You either get to drown slowly as sea levels rise; starve as the sea level forces society inland until the remaining land can't sustain us; burn as the atmosphere is ripped away and temperatures rise till our cells are denatured; or finally, and worryingly more likely, die in riots and fighting over the scarcity of resources.

I hope I'm long dead before this happens.

If this happens it will be the ultimate failure of our species.

If humanity survives this 'slowpocalypse' and somehow finds a copy of this book and reads this, know that all of this could have been averted if we had just thought more macroscopic and long-term as a species.

Why am I writing this doom and gloom?

We need to know our place in the bigger picture.

There are things going on around us that we can't control. There is a load of stuff that is going to happen, and you can't change it.

If you can't change it, don't worry about it.

---

[30] 'Existential climate-related security risk: A scenario approach'. Breakthrough – National Centre for Climate Restoration. https://www.academia.edu/40017142/ Existential_climate-related_security_risk_A_scenario_ approach_THE_AUTHORS Accessed 12/12/19

Be selfish!

RUIN

I don't want to labour this point, but it needs to be said as it is such a big part of our modern society.

"Checks phone for new messages and notifications."

Social media is killing our social lives.

Technology is great. It facilitates so much. It makes our lives simpler. It allows us to keep in touch with people all around the world. We are more connected now than ever before.

Weirdly though, we are isolating ourselves more!

Social media is a one-way filtered window into everyone's lives. The filter isn't just red eye removal and sepia tones; it's a content filter, making sure only the best and most awe-inspiring events make it through.

"Checks phone for new likes and to see if anything has changed."

People typically only post positive and motivational messages and content. We see an amazing world around us. So much happiness. So much joy. So many smiles.

Then we compare it to our own life.

My life looks awful compared to others'.

"It is awful."

The arms race begins!

When something even remotely positive happens, I'll share it. Dress it up attempting to stand out from the in-crowd.

> *"Checks phone and posts comment about reading some great and motivational book by just another guy."*

Peer pressure wins out.

They view it! In their fake voice, with fake emojis, a like or upvote appears and a comment is posted: 'OMG Hun, So jealous! XOXO.'

Moments pass.

They post something. The retaliation has begun. What was originally designed to keep us all connected is now a battlefield of envy, jealousy and bitterness.

It's vile.

It's twisted.

> *"Unfollow. I don't want to hear this anymore."*

It's not going anywhere!

> *"Please follow, like, subscribe, donate, it all really helps! Don't forget to hit that little bell icon to receive notifications of new posts and videos."*

I know lots of people who have completely removed themselves from social media. I envy them. Sadly, as someone who needs to promote themselves, their talks and this book, I must engage with social media.

I really wish I didn't.

> *"Checks phone for new messages and notifications."*

I now post when things are shit. I'd rather be telling people when things are bad and I need help than to only get a response when things are good.

One of my articles, 'Concerning Concern', was written recently whilst I was relapsing into some pretty dark thoughts. It was a piece of absolute misery, but it resonated with readers.

It was a very different way of approaching things.

But people are there and appreciate seeing honesty. People do care. Showing weakness and asking for help does work.

Try it instead of posting that picture of a dessert sometime!

FEUD

Humanity may be one of the most evolved species on the planet, yet we still fight over resources like hyenas over carcasses.

People feel so oppressed, so scared and so ostracised that they feel a need to resort to physical violence. We have situations where knife crimes exists in populated, well-developed cities like London. We have gangs fighting over territory like cats patrolling routes.

There is just too much fighting in the world.

I have appeared on television and radio a few times relating to video games and the impact they are having on the mental health of younger generations.

The first time I appeared on television was related to the addictive nature of loot boxes,[31] randomised virtual content purchased for real money. People likened loot boxes to gambling, which is very fair and reasonable. However, my interviewers immediately jumped from this to whether they should be illegal or strongly regulated. Again, reasonable. The problem is this doesn't address the underlying problem: addiction.

Why do children want to spend all their time in a computer-generated world?

Why do they need to purchase cosmetic items?

Is it to stand out?

Is it to feel special?

Another time, I was asked to pass comment about a doctor who 'prescribed' two weeks away from Fortnite[32] to a child who was showing symptoms of addiction and withdrawal. The host asked me what my thoughts were, and I asked a very simple question in response:

'Do you watch Netflix? Have you ever binge watched a show?'

'Of course,' they answered.

How many of us spent eighteen hours watching a series of 24 to find out how our hero Jack Bauer managed to go

---

[31] https://journals.plos.org/plosone/article?id=10.1371/journal.pone.0213194 Accessed on 06/09/19

[32] www.manchestereveningnews.co.uk/news/parenting/fortnite-addict-prescription-gp-doctor-16058612 Accessed on 06/09/19

an entire day without ever needing the toilet or eating any food?

The host immediately recoiled when I asserted that maybe she should consider herself addicted to Netflix.

She accepted my point begrudgingly.

There are things in games that reinforce addiction: those little dopamine fixes every time a jingle plays, flashes of colour and sound for completing a level, even simply writing 'victory' can reinforce the feeling of success. All these little details are programmed to make you want to come back!

The conversation continued and I was asked about the violence of video games and how it's affecting the youth.

My response?

Have you read the newspapers today? Watched the news? There is death, destruction, murder, rape and even worse all over our media. Which do you think is worse on a child's understanding of whether violence is acceptable? A video game that is moderated by government bodies, has an age classification limiting its purchase, that continually reinforces that it is fictional; or seeing homeless families on the streets dying because of lack of access to medication? How about a family trying to cross the Mexican border and the father drowning as he tries to save his children?

So, when war, death, destruction and fighting are all around us – in our world, in our news and even in our entertainment – don't waste your time fighting with yourself.

It's never worth fighting with yourself!

There is too much hate in the world already.

There's no point hating yourself as well.

Nothing good will ever come from it.

TEND

So, if somehow you manage to stop fighting with yourself and your thoughts,

"Good luck!"

then the only thing left to care for is yourself. This is the message I've been advocating for nine chapters now and will continue advocating in future books and future talks.

"You're committing to these books and talks. I haven't agreed to any of them!"

Listen to yourself.

If you don't want to do something, or something doesn't feel right, don't do it. Talk it through. Figure out what it is you don't want to do and why you don't want to do it.

And then don't fucking do it!

Simple!

Through self-care and understanding, you can become your own best friend. You will be able to support yourself through the bad times but also will be there to celebrate yourself during the good times. You'll be able to keep yourself company when you're lonely and be able to express yourself how you want.

You can do it.

And only you can do it.

You're your own hero.

This is your hero's journey.

It starts now!

Get ready for an adventure.

Get ready for fetch quests and escort missions.

DICK

Remember the words I live by, whatever they mean to you. It's each to their own. It's taken me ages to find something I truly believe in, but now I have it, I'm not letting go.

Don't be a dick and be happy.

If everyone lived by these simple words, I believe worldwide happiness would increase and there would be less fighting and fewer arguments.

Take these words with you to the office. Have your team live by them. Make your boss live by them. Check in with the people around you and find out if they are happy. If you see someone being a dick, stop them.

Build a culture you want to be part of. You can only lead by example and hope others follow. Why should you go first? Because if you don't, nothing will ever change!

I give you full permission to stand up for yourself and take action.

Stop fearing and start feeling.

As you go about finding your happiness and maybe helping others find theirs. Just always remember:

Don't be a dick!

IF YOU WANT TO TALK TO ME

I am not a trained professional in mental health. I am not qualified in anything with regards to mental health. I am just another guy. I have lived with my mental health problem for most of my memorable life and can only talk from a position of experience and wisdom, not of knowledge and understanding.

If you are interested in talking to me about this book, my talks or anything else, please do not hesitate to get in touch with me.

You can reach me on any of the following:

Website   andysalkeld.com
E-mail   info@andysalkeld.com

I cannot promise that I'll respond immediately; but I will do my utmost to respond to you when I get the opportunity.

Thank you for taking the time to read this book.

"I can't believe someone actually made it to the end!"

I look forward to hearing from you.

Andy Salkeld

just another guy

IF YOU WANT TO TALK TO SOMEONE

If you ever reach a point where you think you are considering talking about your mental health and wellbeing, then it is time to start. Don't be scared! Speaking to someone openly and honestly is a sign of real strength and courage; by doing this you are one step closer to understanding yourself.

There are many different people who can help, and it can often be daunting finding out who to talk to first. Below is a list of people and organisations who may be able to help you.

General Practitioner

Your GP, Doctor or Healthcare Professional is often the first person to contact if you feel you might want to talk to someone. Your GP can make a diagnosis, offer you support and/or treatment and potentially refer you to a specialist service. Speak to them openly and honestly, focusing on your feelings and the problems you are experiencing, regardless of size.

National Health Service (NHS)

NHS 111 can help if you or someone you are with has an urgent medical problem and you're not sure what to do. You will be asked to answer questions about your symptoms and a trained adviser will be able to talk you through what to do next.

Telephone   111

Website   111.nhs.uk

Mind

Mind is the leading mental health charity in England and Wales. Mind provide advice and support to empower anyone experiencing a mental health problem. They campaign to improve services, raise awareness and promote understanding. Mind can provide information on a range of topics including: types of mental health problems, where to get help, medication and alternative treatments and advocacy.

Telephone   0300 129 3393

Website   mind.org.uk

Samaritans

Samaritans is a unique charity dedicated to reducing the feelings of isolation and disconnection that can lead to suicide and is available 24/7, before, during and after a crisis. If you need to talk to someone, Samaritans will listen. They will not judge and will not tell you what to do.

Telephone   116 123

Website   samaritans.org

HUCKSTER

KETCHUPS